Confessions

of a **LIP**

READING

Mom

Confessions

of a LIP READING

Mom

SHANNA GROVES

CROSSRIVER

CONFESSIONS OF A LIP READING MOM
Copyright © 2013 Shanna Groves

ISBN: 978-1936501113

For more on Shanna Groves, please visit her website - www.ShannaGroves.com and LipreadingMom.com.

Printed in the United States of America

For my husband and kids, with love.

1 Giving Birth to Confusion

Confession: I don't always listen to doctors.

I gripped the leather armrests and clinched my teeth, horrified at what might happen on the other side of the waiting room. The room was empty and cold.

An ear, nose and throat nurse in milky green scrubs swung open the door.

"Ready?" she said a little too loud, the word over-enunciated.

In her hands was a thin manila file with my name penciled in at the top. New patient forms were tucked inside, with all the sordid details of my health dilemma. When the forms asked for family hearing health history, I was transported to Christmas 1984 in the living room of Grandma and Grandpa Bartlett. A rotary phone, hung on the wood-paneled wall, rang at a deafening pitch. When Grandpa reached to answer, his clam-sized hearing aids brushed against the receiver and whistled like a steam train.

I checked "Yes" next to "history of family hearing loss or deafness."

A doctor in a white lab coat whisked my file from the nurse's hands without looking at her. "So you've been experiencing buzzing noises from inside your ears?" His voice was deep and to the point, a perfect pitch for an army drill sergeant.

Would this be the part when he told me I had cancer?

It had been two months, three weeks, and six days since I noticed the buzzing from inside my ears. Morning, noon, night, locusts buzzed inside my head. I remembered the precise date of my hearing issues because they began the day I gave birth to a healthy seven-pound boy, my firstborn. I was barely twenty-seven years old.

"What you've described is called tinnitus," Dr. Lab Coat said.

After shining a pen-sized flashlight into both my ears, up my nostrils, and down my throat, he jotted notes onto my form. Before I could ask him what kind of cancer tinnitus was, he opened the door and motioned.

"Follow me."

The hallway felt like a page from *The Green Mile*. Florescent lights cast their putrid color on the thin, worn carpet. I marched behind Lab Coat as invisible handcuffs weighed down my arms until they ached.

When he opened another door, I noticed a chair enclosed in a floor-to-ceiling padded mini-room. My high heels dug into the carpet.

Lab Coat pointed to a woman sitting at a desk and waved my file at her.

"New patient," he mouthed to the woman before leaving. She was dressed in normal clothes and wore a plastic smile. In her hands were an enormous set of headphones.

"Put these on," Plastic Smile said as she stepped into the padded mini-room with the chair inside. "Then have a seat."

The mini-room measured no bigger than a coat closet and had a giant window on the wall overlooking Plastic Smile's desk. When I put on the headphones, their bulk covered half my head.

Suddenly, from inside the headphones I heard the flicking

of a switch, followed by a woman's breath.

Plastic Smile tapped on the window. She flashed her mouth full of pearly whites from behind a tabletop microphone stand.

"We're going to do a little test," she said. "It will determine how much loss you have."

My thoughts flashed back to the early 1980s when my kindergarten self did the same type of test.

"Above normal hearing," the doctor had noted. "Just needs to pay attention."

"You know, she almost died as a baby," Mom noted. "Just stopped breathing. Could be a slower learner from the lack of oxygen."

I ignored my thoughts and dug my fingernails into the imaginary electric chair. *Let's hurry and get this over with.* My thoughts drifted to the last time I had felt this anxious.

While trying to get pregnant, I dreamt my baby fell from a ladder.

> *The ladder reached high into the sky. I was at my parent's house and had my new baby, haphazardly showing him off to everyone. The baby was unkempt. He hadn't had a bath in days, but I didn't care, being a mom wasn't my responsibility. I had other things on my mind. Like a hot date with my family to discuss the latest gossip in their lives. Let someone else give him a bath!*
>
> *When it was time to leave my parent's house, I dragged the tiny infant under my arm and hurried to the car. Oh wait — I had something else I had to tell*

Mom before leaving. And then I saw it. The aluminum ladder had several steps on it that practically jutted into the clouds. It stood beside my car, towering over it. It wasn't being used; it was just hanging around.

So this tall, unoccupied ladder looked like a friendly place to lay my child while I went back into the house. Better yet, I could place him on the top step of the ladder so that nothing could harm him. He'd be okay, and I could run inside without having to drag him along.

And I did. I went back in the house, standing with my back against the glass front door. As I turned my head toward the ladder, slowly the ladder lost its balance and swayed on its side until...

A strange-looking guy walked by just in time to grab strands of my baby's hair before he fell to the dirt. And where was I? I was looking through the glass of my parents' front door, watching it all happen.

Even as I analyzed the dream, I wondered how prophetic it was. What was the meaning of the ladder? And why was I such a careless mother?

Could it have been a symbol of my life? The far-reaching goals, the burgeoning career, the nice house in the comfortable suburban neighborhood, the loving husband and the dog that jumped up to see me when I came home from work? The goal of getting through college, attaining that degree, of moving from a small town to the big city, all in pursuit of my ambitions? The timeline to meet that goal, of having a nice office, of achieving some sort of professional respect? Of trying to get pregnant?

My timeline, my ladder was spinning out of control — I

had no way of taking hold of this one aspect of my life and achieving it according to my schedule.

Nine months after the dream, I was an expectant mom. Carrying that child and reflecting on the dream, I wondered where that imaginary ladder was going to take us. Not that I minded being pregnant. It just wasn't something I wanted to endure all my life.

During the first three months, I kept pinching myself, wondering if it was a dream. Then I nearly tripped over the bathroom rug trying to vomit in the commode. Definitely not a dream.

The last three months I spent trying to adapt to life as a weeble wobbler. I felt like a bowling ball with legs trying to make it up and down the stairs without either losing my balance or my bladder. Kind folks told me I had the pregnancy glow. I called it feeling like hell's furnace had been implanted in my body. And I laughed for no reason. How absurd everything was when the only thing that mattered was this little someone inside me who had the hiccups and kicked like crazy on the right side of my stomach.

During the last few moments of baby incubation, my doctor told me the baby was fully developed, just continuing to gain weight. All I knew was my upper right abdomen had gone completely numb and the center of my stomach firm, almost forming a point beneath my oversized T-shirt. And the extremely dry skin on the inside of my thighs could've been marketed to hardware companies everywhere as the latest and greatest sandpaper.

Then there was the shelf. That limited space above the stomach that made a convenient place to keep my idle hands or to prop up my frozen TV dinner while I watched bad reruns.

What a strange, life-changing experience — to be pregnant.

A lot of waiting, wondering, and worrying. I couldn't

predict how, when, or where the baby was actually going to appear. Although, visions of delivering the baby while stuck at a stoplight in rush-hour traffic danced through my head.

Ron and I, like most expectant parents, counted the minutes for our baby to be born. If only my water would break tonight, or I'd develop some real contractions this afternoon, all of our waiting would be over. My husband could've taken his four days off from work, I could've finally started maternity leave from the job I hated, and we could've gotten obligatory phone calls out of the way to our parents.

In the moments just before I became a mom, I carried a mixed bag of emotions. In the hospital delivery room, I lay in a metal bed, gripped the rails, and stared at the gray ceiling. I waited and waited for my baby to be born.

Twenty-one hours later, Nicklaus arrived.

"Would you like to hold him?" the doctor asked.

Suddenly, a ringing bell went off in my ears. "What?" After more questions I couldn't understand, I was taken to a recovery room. A different attending nurse came and went every few hours. They all seemed to mumble, though I tried to listen to their words closely:

"How (ring-ring-ring) are you (ring-ring-ring) feeling?"

"Would you like more (ring-ring-ring) water?"

"How is the (ring-ring-ring) baby nursing?"

"Are you ready for (ring-ring-ring) dinner?"

They cautiously nodded their heads and gave me a brief look that questioned why I wasn't answering all of their questions. Then they explained themselves a little louder.

I was exhausted from the combination of labor and listening to the ringing while every nurse waited for my response.

When everyone left, I gazed at my baby. Smooth pink skin.

Soft tufts of strawberry blond hair. Deep blue eyes squinting at me. His thick lips attached to my left breast. His tiny fingers clenched into fists against my skin. His legs and torso lay cocooned in a delicate blanket at my side. My eyes closed.

I was already eager for the hospital stay to end. No more visiting nurses asking me soft-spoken questions that the ringing noise wouldn't let me hear.

At home, it would be quiet. Peaceful.

2 Why Can't I Hear my Baby?

Confession: I dream about falling asleep.

The ten-week maternity leave was about to end.

"Hon," my Ron called from the front room. "Can you get that?"

I cradled Nicklaus' head to protect his ears when I screamed, "Get WHAT?"

Nicklaus didn't flinch as he continued to nurse. During the day, he spent one hour attached to my bosom; the next hour snoozing at my chest. At night, I'd put him in bed with me to keep up with the on-demand breastfeeding while continuing my shut-eye.

I stroked his feather-soft tuft of strawberry blond hair and breathed in the dreamy scent of Johnson & Johnson baby lotion. I closed my eyes. For a moment, I pictured a warm, beach paradise far away from the snowy gusts of Kansas in January. Hot sand and cool, salty water couldn't have made me as happy as my worn sofa chair and ottoman. It was my blissful cuddling, nursing, and napping spot with Nicklaus.

Loud footsteps pounded toward me. When my eyes popped open, Ron stood over me and Nicklaus, visibly agitated. He handed over the phone. "It's for you. How come you didn't answer it?"

For starters, I wanted to tell him, I'm kinda busy with our portable milk drinker.

"Sorry." I took the phone. "Didn't hear it." I tucked the receiver between my shoulder and ear. "Hello?"

"'hanna? Zat you?" A dull hiss of static filled my ear, making it difficult to determine the caller by voice.

"Who is this?" I said.

More static. "Ha! 'unny girl."

It was a woman's voice. "Honey, who?"

"No, ha ha, no! Iz me. Whatcha doin'?"

I tensed. "What? Could you repeat that? Who is this?"

I heard a confused sigh on the other end, and all chuckling ceased. "SHANNA," the caller said. "IT'S YOUR MOM."

Would life be better if my ears worked the way they were supposed to? I'd been asking myself that question more than once during maternity leave. The stupid hissing sound made my ears act crazy, even in quiet rooms. It sometimes sounded like locusts buzzing or handbells ringing. Or a thousand telephones ringing softly at the same time.

The noise made it tough to hear someone on the phone. Could I notice the subtle differences in people's voices, or the tones used in their speech? Or be able to hear the doorbell ring or the microwave beep, or the wall clock tick with a receiver pushed against my ear? Or distinguish instantly who was calling me by listening to the voice, not merely glancing at caller I.D.?

I was filled with other questions. Would the hissing and buzzing make all other sounds unrecognizable? The sound of my son wailing in his room when I was downstairs? The guitar music Ron strummed behind closed bedroom doors while I stood in the laundry room beside a rumbling dryer? Would I hear Nicklaus' breath as we slept together? His soft cooing?

Maybe I was being punished. I'd been so focused on getting a college degree, landing a high-profile writing job, building a home, and pretending to enjoy my job as a managing editor for a women's magazine. Maybe this was God's way of giving me a spanking. Would I listen to Him, or pay attention to all the other noises coming through my ears? Had I allowed the shouts from family, television, and radio to take priority over God's whispers?

My pain-in-the-ear noise sometimes sounded like birds chirping. On this winter day, as I held my baby and struggled to hear my mom's voice via phone, the bird noise was my music. Except no real birds stayed around these parts of the Midwest when the ground froze and the temps dipped below freezing. Hearing a bird's voice in the winter was a rarity.

As mom attempted to remind me in our phone chat, I must never forget my roots.

"Ya listenin' 'hanna?" she asked. Why couldn't I hear the 'S' in my name?

"Loud and clear, Mom."

I grew up on an Oklahoma farm. From spring through summer, male scissor-tailed flycatchers did their roadside "sky dances." They'd soar one hundred feet into the air in V-shaped flight, then plunge in a zigzag pattern toward the ground. A cackling mating call accompanied their repetitive dance as their scissor tails flapped open and closed. As a child, I remembered how visually and audibly stunning the birds were.

"Ya gettin' much 'leep?" Mom's words were mumbled.

Uh, sleep? "Yeah, whatever."

As a new mom caring for an infant, I hummed songs to lull my baby to sleep. My music was filled with passion but lacking the right pitch. My voice sounded thin, weak. I struggled on the high notes. The unexplained ringing noise inside my ears made the songs sound chaotic. The noise reminded me of the summer's fowl and insect chorus on the Oklahoma farm, and it never quieted, especially as I lay wide awake at night.

"Back to work next week, huh?" Mom said. A rhetorical question, since she'd asked me the same thing yesterday. "I know it's gonna be hard on your budget, 'hanna. But that baby needs his momma."

After the conversation, which I ended abruptly to change Nicklaus' diaper, I closed my eyes and imagined the beach again. This time, it was filled with birds. Their melody of chanting and calling and warbling and trilling played twenty-four hours a day, seven days a week inside my ears. In the warm breezes of a fantasy, in the blowing winds of reality, and in the numbing phone call with my mom. Chirping noise.

My second reason for ending the phone call? I had to get out of my pajamas. A hot pink flannel top and bottoms with penguins on them wouldn't work at the office next week. I'd let myself slip into an eight-to-five schedule of casualness that was about to end. Funny thing was, I never wanted to let myself go this way: the mornings spent watching talk shows and cheesy TV movies in the afternoon, my pixie haircut that needed a trim and highlights two weeks ago, my brown roots spilling out all over the crown of my head. If someone predicted I'd end up a stay-at-home wannabe in my ambitious twenties, I would've rolled my eyes. Me, a 1950s-type house-mommy? Right.

As I rubbed a wet wipe over Nicklaus' bottom, I thought about a notorious former employer who'd kept pestering me about when I would start having babies.

"You're not pregnant, are you?" the boss asked at my job interview. I should've run then.

My face flushed crimson, and sweat beads caused my forehead to glow. "Uh, no." And then, to add fuel to his fire, I said, "Not for another fifteen years, at least."

When Mom found out about my smart-aleck remark, she was convinced Ron and I never would make her and my dad a Grammy and Gramps. Truth was, she only waited a couple of years. I quit just shy of my six-month hiring date. On to the next dream job, where the sheer monotony of my work life drove me to premature pregnancy.

Well, not exactly.

I liked my job okay. Writing for a not-for-profit organizational magazine with a shoestring budget and staff of three was better than unemployment. I traveled throughout the United States to conferences, speaking to women who read the magazine, and posing for pictures with ladies I'd never see again. That college degree in communications prepared me well. I could communicate to strangers, tell them about my glamorous life as a newlywed in the suburbs of Kansas City and the daily antics of my long-haired Chihuahua, who I pretended was my firstborn.

When the dog croaked unexpectedly, I re-examined my goals and realized I wanted more to wake up to in the morning than dog hair and a half-hour work commute. A week later, my home pregnancy test was positive.

"Up you go, Nicklaus." I swept him up into my arms, a fresh diaper on his hiney.

Taking the steps toward his room, I braced myself for what would happen in the next few minutes.

Once inside his room, I gazed at the cheery sunshine yellow walls. Oh, how I'd miss this bright room when the daily grind of work resumed come Monday morning.

We walked to his crib and stood there, admiring the Pottery

Barn bedding I could never afford but a generous relative could and did. Slowly, I lowered Nicklaus into the crib and wrapped the paisley blue and yellow baby quilt over his pajamaed legs.

"You can do this," I told Nicklaus. "Time to nap."

No sooner had I backed away ten steps than his whimpering started.

"It's okay," I said to him.

I eased myself out of the doorway. That's when Nicklaus' full-on wailing began. I started to shut the door and the crying intensified.

The noise messed with my ears. What I heard was "WAH-HH! (Ring-ring-ring!) WAHHH! (Chirp-chirp-chirp!) WAH-HH! (Buzz-buzz-buzz!)"

It's okay. I can do this. Don't give in. Don't go get him.

I closed the door and walked as fast as I could down the stairs. When I reached the bottom, I couldn't hear Nicklaus anymore. He was still crying, I guessed, but I couldn't hear him.

Downstairs, all was as quiet as before.

⁓

Five days later, as I drove through the evening rush-hour traffic, the sky was beginning to darken. When I'd left for work that morning, the last stars faded into the horizon.

The smell of grilled chicken and veggies filled the kitchen. Ron's job was closer to the babysitter's, so he had already made it home with Nicklaus when I walked through the door.

"How was it?" Ron mumbled, facing the stove. "Good day?"

My attention was elsewhere, fixed on Nicklaus who sat buckled in his car seat. It rested on top of the kitchen table. He gnawed at his tiny fist, a sign that he was hungry.

Without missing a beat, I unbuckled him, then swooped him out of the seat.

I carried him to my favorite sofa chair and ottoman, sat down, and raised up my shirt.

"Here you go, little guy," I said.

As he nursed, I breathed in his delicious baby lotion smell and stroked his hair, which had begun to darken.

Just the week before, I had left him in his crib, and he wailed for an hour. Ron had told me how long Nicklaus cried since I couldn't hear from downstairs. The next day, Nicklaus cried maybe fifteen minutes. The following day, he went right to sleep.

That night I decided that, come nighttime, I would tuck him into bed right beside me. Then I could feel his quiet breath against my skin, even if I couldn't hear it. I had missed Nicklaus, and I didn't want to be away from my baby.

Not at night, not during the day, not ever.

3 Conference Calls and Terrible Twos

Confession: My office has toilet paper.

Thanks to a tire blowout, I was late to my son's first birthday party.

I was on my way home from work and it delayed my arrival by two hours. If a Good Samaritan hadn't pulled over and helped put on the spare, I would have spent the night in my little Honda.

I pulled into the driveway with just enough time to add "Happy Birthday Nicklaus" in icing to the cake before he blew out his candle. My in-laws, who traveled five hours on the interstate, beat me to the party by an hour.

"You okay, Shanna?" Ron asked as I held back tears. It was pitch dark when I left for work that day, and the sky was black now. How much time would I have with my boy before I tucked him into his own little bed? An hour-and-a-half.

Quitting work to stay at home with Nicklaus wasn't a financial option. I knew very few women who didn't work outside of the home. Two-income families were a vivid reality within my circle of co-workers and friends.

Before Nicklaus' birth, the choice had been made: I would never stay at home. And I knew being confined to a home-based job would be very boring and, at times, stressful. I mean, to whom would I vent when deadlines mounted and I was frazzled?

Then it happened. My son's birth. Maternity leave. Ten weeks of staying at home. As I held this beautiful little boy with strawberry blond hair and eyes shaped like Ron's, I started to envision being with him. All the time.

I started doing the math. With my income and Ron's, we lived comfortably. Enough to eat out two to three times a week. Without my income finances would be tight. There was no way we could survive on one salary alone.

My head said, "You have to go back to work. How are you going to pay the bills?" My heart screamed, "Look at this little boy. Surely you can find a way to stay home with him."

I called two of the only mom friends I knew who didn't work outside the home. One friend suggested I read how-to books for wannabe stay-at-home moms. It inspired me to give up my credit card and shop the dollar stores. It also pointed a finger at all the designer baby clothes and eating out a dozen times a month. My other friend said she would pray for me. What, that's it?

After maternity leave, I went back to work. Not because I wanted to, but for economic purposes. As I sat at my desk at work each morning, I thought about my son. I wondered what new things he was doing and if he was saying a new word or smiling for the first time. I plastered my desk with pictures of him. And I called the sitter at least once a day to see what Nicklaus was up to. Uh, sleeping in a baby swing?

A few weeks earlier, on my way to pick Nicklaus up from day-care, I got stuck in heavy traffic. I panicked. The day care closed at six o'clock and traffic crept along like a row of shiny turtles.

Finally, I made it through the bumper-to-bumper cars, and

pulled into the daycare, right at six. Nicklaus was the only child left, and it was almost dark outside.

Where had the day gone? I would only have two hours with my son before he went to sleep that night.

Now, as I looked at Nicklaus with baby blue frosting smeared across his cheeks, I made up my mind. I would find a way to stay home with him.

My first phone call was to the credit card company.

"Hello, sir, I'd like to cancel my Visa card."

"What (hiss-hiss-hiss) is (buzz-buzz-buzz) your (ring-ring-ring)..." The Visa rep apparently spoke English as a second language.

"My what?" I said.

"Your (hiss-hiss-hiss) crett cawd numb?"

"My WHAT?"

Oh, credit card number.

"Yes, it's..." I lowered the phone. "Wait a sec. Just need to dig through my purse here. Oh man, there's that bag of cereal Nicklaus lost. Wallet, wallet, where are you? And there's my receipt from yesterday. I spent how much at that restaurant?"

I seriously had a problem, not counting the clutter in my bag. If I couldn't keep track of expenses on two incomes, how would I be an expert with one? And why couldn't I make a phone call without having to ask "Huh? What'd you say?" fifteen times?

Click. Hang up. Try again later.

Thus began my search for various work-at-home options, preferably ones that required limited use of a telephone. Make-up sales. Jewelry get-togethers. Scented lotion spa parties.

"Would you like to try this lotion?" I asked a friend. "It'll make your skin feel so soft and..."

Suddenly, my friend's hand turned splotchy purple where

I'd been rubbing the cream.

"How about this jewelry?" I asked Friend Number Two. "This necklace will look darling with your blouse."

Out popped the center stone in her necklace before I could find the warranty.

"Would you like to try some of this eye shadow? This mascara? This eau-de-toilette, however-it's-pronounced-perfume?" I couldn't sell aspirin to a migraine sufferer. I wasn't enthusiastic or pushy enough, but I kept searching for the perfect job.

"My boss is looking for someone to type his notes," Friend Number Three said. "He'll provide you with everything you need to get started, and he'll pay what you ask." Sign me up!

I spent the next evening working at my new work-at-home job in my comfy home office making twenty-five dollars an hour, big bucks for an aspiring mom-preneur. The catch: I had to type more than forty-five words a minute from a dictating machine, complete with headphones and a foot pedal that controlled the dictation machine.

Friend Number Three's boss' voice blasted through my headphones as I attempted to type: "Note to self: Make sure to hire a typist who can hear as well as she types." What?

My fingers danced across the keyboard in time with the words I struggled to hear via headphones.

SALES PROJECT XXXX (couldn't hear words clearly) WAS A SUCCESS. I NEED TO NOTE FOLLOWING THINGS... NUMBER ONE: XXXX (nope, couldn't hear that). TWO: (still can't hear). THREE: (I think I need to find a new job).

I wanted so desperately to work at home, within an arm's reach of my now active toddler. I wanted to eat lunch with him in our kitchen, instead of take-out in a cubicle with all the other working moms. I wanted to sing him to sleep at nap time and take a nap myself. I wanted to find a job that didn't require me to use my hissing, buzzing, screwed-up ears. I wanted to enclose myself in a bubble. Me, Nicklaus, a paycheck, and my penguin PJs. A new set of ears would've been icing on the dreamy cake.

The computer became a refuge for all these thoughts. As I contemplated imminent death by scented spa lotion parties or imagined choking myself with a necklace missing its stone, my hands flew across the keyboard. I came up with a brilliant book idea — "A Day in the Life of a Wannabe Stay-at-Home Mommy."

Mommy Tale Number One: I love holding my baby until he falls asleep. Okay, he's not a baby, and he's not really falling asleep. Wait...Where's that snore coming from?

Mommy Tale Number Two: This massive headache won't go away. I tried taking two aspirin and waiting twenty minutes. Nothing. I tried taking a soothing bath, but then chucked that idea when I couldn't fit my whole bloated self in the tub with all of Nicklaus' floaty toys. I think I'll sleep. Yep, that will help. Do you think my boss will notice?

Mommy Tale Number Three: I wonder what Nicklaus is doing at day care. I wonder who is feeding him breakfast right now. I wonder who will change his diaper afterward. I wonder how long he will nap or if he will nap at all. I wonder if his cough has gotten better. The doctor said Nicklaus wouldn't be contagious after twenty-four hours of medicine. Do twenty-one and a half hours count? I didn't want to go to work, but I used up all my paid time off for Christmas and Nicklaus' birthday. Darn rules. I wonder if I can break them just this one time.

Mommy Tale Number Four: Okay, I'm having a meltdown right now. Nicklaus pulled a crock pot on top of his head. My back was turned just a second to get something out of the stove, and BOOM! Down with the slow cooker full of cooked pot roast. The cord had dangled just enough for him to grab it and pull it off the counter. Nicklaus fell. Slow cooker busted. Food splattered all over him. His head was cut. Blood. Rag, where's a rag? Blood. Stop bleeding! It's okay, baby, Mommy's here. Crying. His tears. My tears. Oh, Lord, what have I done?

Mommy Tale Number Five: Thank goodness Ron was home so I didn't have to call the ambulance. Nicklaus lay in my lap with a towel to his forehead while Ron drove fast. The ER doors swung open as my feet slid across the cold, hard floor. The check-in receptionist noticed the bloody towel and my white face and shoved the patient clipboard into Ron's hands. "Sign this and this, and we'll get him into a room."

The kind receptionist's eyes never left mine. "What happened?" Her voice was gentle while I stifled back more tears.

"I. He. Slow. Cook!" I cried on the receptionist's shoulder.

We waited for the doctor, then we waited for the numbing medicine to take effect on Nicklaus' forehead. I watched as two nurses and the doctor struggled to wrap him in a mini-straightjacket so he wouldn't move during the procedure. He screamed. One stitch. Two stitches. More screaming as I cupped his tiny face in my hands. Three stitches in his forehead just below his hairline. And that was it.

Mommy Tale Number Six: I wish I hadn't stopped breast-feeding. Yes, it was exhausting. I had to carry a breast pump briefcase to work and put a "Do Not Disturb" sticky note on the door three times a workday to use the blasted thing. Pump-SWISH!-Pump-SWISH! And I produced one bottle of mommy milk a day. One measly bottle after fifteen minutes of pumping each side while trying to type on the work computer or make phone calls, door still closed. I didn't produce enough to feed my baby. At one week old, he was getting a supplemental bottle of formula. By six months of age, most of his nutrition came from Enfamil, not me. Over a holiday weekend, I decided to wean him cold turkey. It was awful. He wanted to nurse to fall asleep, and I listened to him cry. I was painfully engorged, couldn't nurse, and cried. Awful.

Mommy Tale Number Seven: I keep thinking about what that doctor told me. "Shanna, you're going deaf." No, not those exact words.

"You've got progressive hearing loss," he said. "You need hearing aids."

What is PHL (my silly acronym)?

"It's the sensorineural loss of your hearing at a progressive rate."

Huh?

"Some of the nerves inside your inner ear have been destroyed. Not sure why. That's why you hear the ringing, which we call tinnitus."

Oh, no. The cancer. "Tin-night-us?"

"It means your ears can't hear all the high frequency sounds anymore so they are struggling to process sound. That's what makes the ringing sound in your ears."

So tin-night-us isn't cancer, and it's caused by hearing loss?

"Will the ringing ever stop?" I asked.

He shook his head. "Probably not."

It took fourteen months, three weeks, and two days for my dream to come true. I became a stay-at-home mommy. Actually, a mommy who stays at home with her child and works part-part-part time. I also watched a houseful of other people's children.

As my foray into staying at home, I started a licensed in-home day care. Watching other people's kids could provide Nicklaus with playmates and me with a paycheck. Easy enough.

"Nicklaus did WHAT?" Mom shouted into the phone.

"He bit the kid," I said.

"WHICH kid?"

"The three-year-old I watch."

"Well, WHERE did he bite him?"

I paused to collect my rattled thoughts.

"On the arm. And the cheek. And the hand. And the..." I glared at Nicklaus standing in the corner of the living room. His time-out corner.

"Good grief, Shanna! WHY are you doing this?" Mom asked.

Why was I watching other people's kids when Nicklaus had a biting problem and wouldn't share his toys, and I hadn't taken a shower that morning?

I'd passed all the safety inspections. My day care license hung proudly on the refrigerator with ABC magnets surrounding it. I'd borrowed a double stroller to take the little ones on beautiful spring day walks. I typed an activity agenda for the day care parents to read each morning. Yet on half of those agendas, one biting incident was reported. My son's biting incident.

The moms and dads were fine with the first and second bitings. Boys will be boys. He's teething. He likes to put things in his mouth. After the sixth and seventh bite reports, the parents feared dropping their children off at my house each morning. Would their children survive Nicklaus "Jaws" Groves?

When I made the dubious choice to haul the kids, including a newborn, to the swimming pool on a field trip, I was in the thick of Wrestling Biting Slamdowns.

"Nicklaus, don't bite," I told him. "Nicklaus, Nick — you get back here right now and tell him you're sorry. Is your finger okay? I know it hurts. I'm so sorry you got bit. NICKLAUS!"

At the end of the year, I officially retired as Stay-at-Home Biting Day Care Licensee.

Ron and I still needed paychecks, but now I had four of them. While Nicklaus pierced other kids' skin with his teeth, I brainstormed other work-at-home options. The answer came to me while I was sitting on the toilet.

"Do you want to write for us from home?" My ex-boss' voice sounded upbeat.

I was tired. "When can I start?"

Within a week, I was juggling Ex-Boss' assignment; plus, another two I snagged as a freelancer for the local newspaper. I also had my Mommy Tales to keep me busy. What started as my journal about being Nicklaus' mom became a website and e-newsletter with a loyal readership. I even had advertisers.

Why had I never thought of it before? I had heard of successful freelance writers who wrote for magazines, newspapers and other businesses. Their names were Dave Barry, Billy Graham, and Dear Abby. Not me.

After the final biting incident that resulted in teeth marks on his face, I decided writing would be the right work-at-home option for me.

I whipped out the only credit card I never shredded and invested in a new home computer and business cards. I dedicated my cell phone as a business line. I subscribed to writing e-newsletters and discovered interesting opportunities. "Do you want to write about breast cancer?" Sure! Reclaimed building supplies? Absolutely! Potty training? Uh...

I typed query letters and made photocopies of my writing samples. Then I started submitting letters and samples to a dozen different publications.

Within a couple of months, I heard from a major newspaper. Surprisingly, they were short on freelance writers at the time and desperately needed new writing talent. Why they hadn't called Dave Barry, I'll never know.

I got my first assignment from that newspaper within a month. After seeing my name in print, I experienced a self-confidence boost.

"Look, Nicklaus. My name is in print." I shoved the newspaper in his face. "No... Don't bite."

I got the courage to contact another former employer, a magazine, and they began giving me assignments. It was the boss who asked me all those years before when I would get pregnant. Well, guess what, buddy boy? I already did!

Slowly but surely, the freelancing world came to life. My office was often the bathroom, a closet, and the back porch because these were the quietest spots to make phone calls. No caller could hear Nicklaus banging his little fist against the closet door, if I held two pillows over the phone to muffle background noise.

It was still tricky making all those phone calls to conduct interviews, but I wasn't going to let that stop me. While the caller talked into the receiver, my fingers flew across the keyboard at a rapid pace, hoping to catch their every word on the computer. Toward the end of the call, I read back the typed notes verbatim so the person could confirm whether or not he'd been quoted accurately. It worked like a charm.

One year and three months after my son's birth, I finally got to stay home with him. It wasn't perfect, but it was a start. I watched Nicklaus during the day, made calls during nap times, and worked on writing assignments on nights and weekends.

It was a constant juggle, but I was home — with my child. I got to eat breakfast, lunch and dinner with him, watch him play outside in our backyard on warm, spring afternoons. I became more engaged with my precocious little biter.

One night, I tiptoed into his room at midnight after completing a work deadline. As he slept, I watched him. I couldn't hear him breathing, but I shrugged that off.

My boy and I were home.

4 A Haircut Away from Perfection

Confession: No Twiggy haircut for me.

The longer I lived the life of a work-at-home mommy, the longer my hair grew.

When I left full-time work, I had a haircut as short as Chynna Phillips during her Wilson Phillips' days. It was shaved in the back with long bangs in front and spiky hair at the crown. Throw on a mini-skirt and go-go boots, and I would've looked like Twiggy's ugly baby sister.

Since Ron and I were on a budget, it made sense to skip the $75 a month designer haircuts. Goodbye, Salon Sassy. Hello, Really Cheap Cuts.

"Sit still." I held Nicklaus in my lap while the fresh-out-of-beauty-school hairstylist trimmed both of our bangs. Spritz, spritz, spritz went her spray bottle, dusting our hair and faces with water droplets.

"Ahhhh, no want!" Nicklaus fidgeted with each spray.

"Hold still," I said as I tried to spit out the piece of Nicklaus' cut hair caught on my tongue.

The lollipop reward couldn't have come faster. While he sat blissfully on the waiting room carpet with a grape sucker jammed in his mouth, I brushed what remained of his baby hair off my sweater.

"How do ya want zee hair trimmed, miss?" The stylist said through her thick Russian accent.

My ears strained to hear her words. Was she asking me about my hair, Nicklaus' hair, or the weather?

"Just trim up the bangs, please," I said. "I'm letting the layers in back grow out."

Thick Russian Accent asked me a question I didn't understand.

"Sure." I smiled. "Okay." I had no idea what she had asked, but she seemed nice. What difference did it make what she said?

While she clipped away at the strands that fell below my eyebrows, I tried to empty my mind of racing thoughts. Being a mom of an active toddler required the patience of a grandma and the energy of a teenager. My feet were cracked and blistered from standing all day, running around chasing my boy outside, or going for walks pushing the stroller in one hand and yanking my dog's leash with the other.

I had gone from a sit-in-a-cubicle-all-day job to running marathons at the parks when Nicklaus took off and hid. When I found him, Nicklaus had either swallowed sand, pooped in his diaper and smeared it on his backside, or bit an unassuming child on the arm. I knew he was nearby if I heard another child's piercing cries of "Mommy! He bit me!"

Then I thought about my hair. It had been snipped short before I got pregnant, thanks to my scissor-happy, fresh-out-of-beauty-school younger sister, Janie. Every time I saw her, Janie treated me either to a fresh haircut, eyebrow tease, or total restyle. That is, when she wasn't plucking out her own eyebrows, bleaching her hair platinum blonde with reddish streaks or getting a paisley tattoo etched on her stomach.

I had Janie to thank for my newly acquired fashion sense. Hello, bargain-rack sheer tops and chunky high heels. My yearnings for the hippest hairdo the discount haircut shops could offer also were attributed to my sister's influence.

With each snip at my bangs, I imagined myself in Janie's beauty shop back in Podunk, Oklahoma, with The Who or The Doors blaring on the radio. Man, I loved her retro-punk style.

"Ya like?" Thick Russian Accent said as she whirled my chair around to face the mirror and flashed a confident smile.

I stared at my reflection. Oh. My. Word! Not only were my bangs an inch shorter than they'd ever been, but the layers in back had been brushed away from my ears and tucked behind them, flipping up at the ends. Could you say, "Bad haircut from 1962?"

The style made my jawline squarish while the flip-thing made the whole lower half look like a rigged box. The bangs were chopped so high, I could count all the wrinkles in my young forehead. As I grimaced at my mirrored self, I counted... One. Two. Three. Four. Five...

"Ya no like?" Thick Russian Accent asked, her smile melting.

I glared at my hair flips tucked behind exposed ears and remembered how much I hated this part of my anatomy. My highly visible, messed-up, ringing-24/7 ears. I imagined wearing some obnoxious ear doodads like the hearing aid guy had tried to sell me the year before. Not a flattering haircut anyway, but what would it look like with behind-the-ear hearing aids plugged into my visible ears like electrical cords?

Truth be told, I was beginning to see the validity in those hearing aids. I could no longer hear my phone ring. The kitchen stove timer beeped five minutes before I realized it and turned the oven off. Door bells went unheard. My son's nighttime cries from behind his bedroom door were silenced.

Ring-ring-ring. Buzz-buzz-buzz. Those were the ear sounds

that greeted me like an alarm clock each morning. At night, my ears serenaded me with cricket choirs and chiming handbells.

I could no longer participate in pillow talk with Ron after the lights were dimmed. Often, I lay with my ear pressed against his cheek so I could feel the vibrations of his voice. Soothing, but not easily understood.

"We finished?" Thick Russian Accent unsnapped the cape around my shoulders covered in snippets of hair.

I reached for the hair she had tucked behind my ears and let it fall free. The strands stroked my jawline. My new hairstyle looked like it belonged on an old British TV spy show.

Thick Russian Accent nodded and smiled. "Ya do like?"

I paid the check, left a modest tip, and whisked Nicklaus off the floor. He had the sucker stick in his mouth, chewing on it like gum. Before I could pry it out, he swallowed it.

Back in the car, I debated making the call. It was difficult to hear well on a cell phone with Nicklaus squirming in the backseat, but I knew the longer I waited, the easier it was to avoid.

"Dr. Wilson's office," the receptionist answered. "How may I direct your call?"

Nicklaus fidgeted with one of his backseat toys. I cupped my phone-free ear to block out his white noise.

"I need to make an appointment. About hearing aids." The words flew out of my mouth in one breathless plea. "I really need them."

Phone Receptionist paused. Was that a sigh I heard?

"Have you been referred?" she said. "You must have your family doctor refer you. Because insurance won't cover it if we don't have a referral."

Insurance hadn't wanted to cover hearing aids when I'd first visited Dr. Wilson. When I sat in that space-age sound booth and listened to beeps through headphones two years before. That appointment confirmed I didn't have any trace of ear cancer.

"I know all that. I'll pay whatever," I said.

Phone Receptionist said nothing. Meanwhile Nicklaus pushed the buttons on his twinkle-twinkle-little-star music box.

Twinkle, twinkle, little...

"I'm not following you," said the receptionist with a hint of sarcasm that I detected, hard of hearing or not.

Up above the world so...

"We can only see you and insurance will only cover your appointment by referral," she said.

Twinkle, twinkle, little...

"So you can't even see me unless my family doctor refers me? Because of insurance? Is that what you mean?" I said.

...How I wonder what you are.

"Right."

Beautiful. Why were these behind-the-ear devices, so essential to my way of life, such a financial headache?

When the audiologist tried to sell me a set of digital hearing aids, the $5,000 fee didn't just include the contraptions worn behind the ears. A bundling of services were included with that price tag — annual or semiannual hearing tests, professional fittings with an audiologist, computer programming of the aids by an audiologist, and minor in-office hearing aid repairs.

Did that justify paying thousands of dollars on digital gadgets small enough to fit in my two-year-old boy's pudgy hands? How could people afford hearing aids if they didn't have insurance coverage or credit cards?

No magic fairy waved a wand over a silently suffering hard-of-hearing mom and granted her the wish of free hearing aids. No audiologist awarded her patience with complimentary hearing devices. No legislator took money out of his or her checking account and sent that mom a check to cover her audiologist bill. How could a mom be free to hear her child's voice without the means to pay for her listening ability?

I was stuck; unable to purchase hearing aids because I couldn't get insurance to approve my appointment or help pay for them. If I suffered from a debilitating disease, some doctor, charity or Good Samaritan would come to my rescue and raise funds in my time of medical need.

Not yours truly. I strained to hear my son and worried about the demands of a job that required good phone hearing ability. How much longer could I seamlessly function in a world becoming softer to my ears?

I finally swallowed my pride and accepted reality — my hearing ability wasn't getting better. I desperately needed hearing aids. No longer in denial, it became my habit to strike up a conversation with anyone who would listen to my slowly-going-deaf story...at the grocery store, church, gym, or library. If my hearing made an activity difficult, I spoke up.

While my almost three-year-old boy yelled "Mama!" at a deafening pitch, I pulled a woman working in the library aside and told her why he screeched at me.

"I'm hard of hearing," I said. "He talks loud so I can hear him."

The lady turned from her desk. After a short pause, I expected her to offer a sympathetic, "Oh, I'm sorry. I had no idea."

Instead, she pulled something out of her ear. "I wear this," she said, holding a tiny, in-the-canal hearing aid. I was intrigued. This woman seemed so young.

She told me that her kids, although older than mine, also tended to talk loud with her. It became a show-and-tell of hearing-loss stories.

"They scream all the time."

"They do?" I asked her.

"When my back is turned, in the car, whenever I cannot see them. They scream to get my attention."

This woman, in her forties and only a decade older than me, got it. She understood what life was like while treading the uncertain waters of hearing loss. The librarian knew that a loud child wasn't being intentionally disruptive.

"Thanks for telling me," she said. "About your hearing loss."

I shrugged off yet another one of my son's yells. "Better that you know than think my child is just a brat."

Then my little boy and I, with his too-shrill-for-the-library voice, got the heck out of there.

⁓

Screaming child or not, I could not understand the chatter and babbling coming out of Nicklaus' mouth. How could I lip-read a child who didn't know how to enunciate his words, look at me when he spoke, or who stuck toys in his mouth while chatting away?

On a typical day, by noon I had only clearly understood about sixty percent of what he said. Since he wasn't old enough to write his words, I tried to interpret a preschooler's gaagaa-googoo language. So, I got creative. Moms who lip-read need to think outside the box. Solution — play word games.

One day, I rounded up Nicklaus' favorite toys, including the entire *Toy Story* family.

ME: (pointing to Buzz Lightyear) "Who's that?"

NICKLAUS: (trying to put Buzz's wingtip in his mouth) "No more plaaaaaay."

Maybe I needed another strategy.

ME: (texting Ron at nine o'clock in the morning) "Little Guy misses Daddy. When U coming home?"

5 This Mommy Has to Toughen Up

Confession: I'm a people-pleasing addict in recovery.

As soon as I pushed out Nicklaus in the delivery room, my ears rang.

The epidural was so strong, I forced myself to push without feeling a thing. On a scale from one to ten, my labor and delivery pains were at a zero. Since a mirror hung over us, I watched my face turn a sweaty beet red with each push. I smiled at my reflection.

My OB couldn't believe I didn't flinch when she performed an emergency episiotomy. No mom who's dilated to a ten with a baby's head crowning has a reason to laugh. I did because I couldn't feel a thing.

I thought about my pain-free delivery as I sat in Dr. Wilson's office. Two years after the initial consultation for hearing aids, there I was finally purchasing them.

My ear problems started after delivering Nicklaus. In the moments when I nursed Nicklaus in the delivery room, the experience was anything but quiet. My ears squealed, buzzed, and rang at a deafening pitch. I thought it was ear wax buildup. Dad once went to a doctor who used a sharp, pointy instrument to dig out his earwax. After getting the gunk out, my Dad was fine.

After getting the office visit referral hassle taken care of — which consisted of multiple phone calls to my insurance company, family doctor, and Dr. Wilson's receptionist — I was ready for my hearing aids. Like plugging in an electric cord and flipping the switch, I hoped all my problems would be solved with hearing aids plugged into my ears.

"This will feel cold." Dr. Wilson's hearing aid dispenser, Denny Knotts, held what looked like a cake decorating tool.

I sat in the leather chair across from Denny, Ron by my side. The only sounds I heard, other than tinnitus, was my rapid breath. Was "cold" a metaphor for pain?

Denny tucked the tool into my left ear. With a long squeeze, out squirted purplish goop that filled the hole of my ear. It chilled my skin.

"We're making an impression of your ear." Denny said while he squeezed. "For the ear mold."

Impression? Mold? The only impression I had at the moment was of terror. I envisioned a flesh-eating mold sucking the life and tinnitus out of my ear.

Denny pulled the tool away, and I sat with ice-cold goop in my ear, wondering when my skin would begin rotting.

"Alrighty. Ready for the next ear?" he said.

Not only was the ear mold stuff uncomfortable, but his words were muffled out of this clogged-up ear. My left ear had the least hearing loss, according to Dr. Wilson's tests before. I used my left ear for making phone calls, for listening to Nicklaus' toddler voice, for hearing people's voices.

Denny's question now sounded like, "Ah. Read' ne' r'?"

I put my lip-reading skills to work, to no avail. "Uh, could you repeat that?"

Denny gazed into my eyes and said, with the clearest enunciation known to hard-of-hearing man, "Are. You. Rea-dy. For. The. Next. Ear?"

I nodded, and the cake-decorating-like tool found my right ear. My bad ear, the one that heard ten percent less than the other one. I struggled to hear anyone and anything while driving because my bad right ear faced everyone. My left ear, the good one, heard nothing but wind noise coming from the driver's side window.

Squirt. Blop. Now both of my ears were clogged with gunk. So this is what a deaf person's life was like. As the purplish goo hardened inside each ear, Denny bantered.

"Are you excited about your hearing aids?" he said.

What I heard, "R 'ou 'ted 'bow ear ad?"

"Could you repeat that?" I said.

Ron tapped my shouldered.

"HE. SAID. ARE. YOU. EX-CI-TED. A-BOUT. YOUR. HEAR-ING. AIDS?"

I nodded, although secretly I had another adjective for this whole experience. It wasn't an appropriate word to speak out loud. And why was Ron talking with exaggerated lips, speaking his words as if swimming in ocean water without a snorkel on?

I felt like a kindergartener once again. Overwhelmed, terrified, and unable to understand a word the teacher was saying.

Once, at age six, I had my ears tested because I struggled in reading circle. A group of us sat at a table, wearing headphones, with worksheets in front of us. Each time we heard a question via headphones, we were supposed to write the appropriate response on the sheet. I sat there, perplexed. Was I supposed to be hearing a question?

My parents sought out the most respected children's audiologist in Oklahoma. After listening to a series of beeps and spoken words, the audiologist's conclusion was that my hearing was above normal. I simply had trouble paying attention.

"Huh?" I struggled to hear Denny's series of questions. Did he just say I would look great in my new hearing aids or that he had developed a cure for AIDS?

Ron tapped my shoulder. "HE. ASKED. IF. YOU. WERE. REA-DY. TO. TAKE. OUT. THE. EAR. IM-PRESS-IONS."

I nodded, closed my eyes. If the purplish stuff felt uncomfortable going in my ears, how would it feel coming out?

"O-kay." Denny was close enough, I felt his breath on my left cheek. "One. Two. Three."

He pulled the impression out, and I could hear the office's air conditioner humming once again.

"Are. You. O-kay?" Denny's voice was unbelievably articulate and loud.

"Uh, sure." I didn't feel so much as a tickle as the impression exited my ear.

Denny held a purplish rendition of what my left ear mold looked like: the small circular ear opening and the cartilage around the hole. It looked like a leftover body part from the *Star Wars* special effects department.

"Ready. For. The. Next. Ear?" Denny attempted a smile.

Every time he uttered his robotic words, spit sprayed out of his mouth.

"O-kay." If he was going to over-enunciate, so was I.

With the right ear impression out, I heard the air conditioner humming and the sound of heels clanking against the linoleum floors in the hallway behind the door.

Denny held my fake ears in all their sci-fi glory.

"We'll. Send. These. Off. To. The. Lab. And. Have. Your.

Hear-ing. Aids. Ready. Next. Week. O-kay?"

I was glad to hear anything but garbled words. My few mo-ments with true deafness were over. Thank God.

"O-kay," I said.

I whipped out my credit card faster than Luke Skywalker handled his laser. It was the only way to pay for my out-of-this-world, and out-of-my-budget hearing aids. My insurance company dropped the ball on this necessity. It didn't fork over a dime in reimbursement.

Denny handed over the bill. In one column were the charges for my left hearing aid; in the other column, the right. I didn't understand why Denny had typed up a line-by-line ex-planation of expenses, when I knew everything was way over my spending limit.

How many people forked over five grand on a set of devices that were worn in the ear like medical jewelry? I spent less on my TVs and kitchen appliances combined.

"Y'know, there's a great organization that can help you," Denny said over his shoulder after whisking away my credit card. "It's called SHHH."

I leaned in closer to see his mouth. Did he just tell me to shut up? Denny turned, half-smiled, then moved his lips slower than humanly possible. "SHHH. As. In. Self. Help. For. Hard. Of. Hear-ing."

I still hadn't heard the "SHHH" part clearly. Anyone with my kind of hearing loss struggled with high-frequency conso-nant sounds, particularly "S" and "Sh." Denny's "SHHH" was only a whisper-soft noise flowing through my flawed ears.

"It's. A. Sup-port. Group. For. Hard. Of. Hear-ing. Peo-ple," Denny said. "Like. You."

Like me. How did Denny, who talked like Mr. Roboto,

know anything about me?

SHHH — the acronym my ears couldn't hear — was likely another venture I couldn't afford. My credit card and level of hearing loss acceptance were just about maxed out.

"Guess I'll check it out then," I said, gritting my teeth.

⁓

A week later, I plugged in my new set of ears. The first thing I heard was Denny's excruciatingly over-enunciated, "What. Do. You. Think?"

I heard his raspy breath, his phlegmy cough. The AC units hummed like screeching birds, and someone's heels clanked against the linoleum hallway floors behind his door.

"Uh, can we turn the volume down a bit?" My voice had an echo. "Can-an, we-ee, turn-urn, the-e, vol'-ol', 'ume-'ume, down-own, a bit-it?"

The hearing aids fit in the palm of each hand. They were crescent-shaped, like moon slivers peeking from behind clouds. The outside shell was the color of warm oatmeal. A skinny, clear tube jutted out of each shell and connected to a clear oval mold specially designed to fit in my ear. The molds rubbed against the skin surrounding my ear holes, and the shells pressed against the cartilage.

The sound of Denny's articulated words competed with my pulse beating in each ear.

"Is. That. Better?" He fiddled with some keys on his key-board. My hearing aids were connected to his computer via a thin extension cord plugged into the back of each ear shell.

I listened to his fingers tap-tap-tap at the keys. Ron, sit-ting beside me, patted my back and shoulders. The AC noise quieted to a moderate hum.

"I think-ink so-oo." It sounded like I was speaking into a microphone and projecting my voice across the office. And my voice sounded tinny. Whiny.

I stepped into a parking lot full of "zooms" and "roars."

"Where's that sound coming from?" I asked Ron.

Parking lot engines clanked into ignition, and gas pedals went vroom-vroom as if taking off on the Indy 500. In the distance, I heard heart-stopping ambulances squealing to unknown places. My ears hadn't heard this much noise since grade school, when I sat on a bus full of classmates.

Inside the car, I found a moment of silent refuge. What had all that obnoxious noise been? The hearing aids amplified everything, even the plink-plink sound of my eyes blinking and the puffs of my breath.

Ron slammed his door a little too hard in our tiny Honda. The keys rattled against the ignition. His foot pumped the gas, his strong arm popped the gear shift back, and his shoe pounded the gas pedal. The tires scratched the pavement and I heard the cracking of loose gravel hitting the wheels beneath us.

Even with the windows rolled up and the AC blasting, I heard outside wind hissing at me. Then, Ron switched on a classic rock station, and I got more than an earful of Led Zeppelin guitar wailing.

With nowhere to hide, I retreated to the only spot where I could find tranquility — my imagination. I was on a bus bursting at the seams with elementary school animals. The bus bully throwing spit wads into my hair. My sister Janie singing the Smurfs' "La-La-La-La-La-La Happy Song" to make me laugh.

I gritted my teeth.

Turn. This. Racket. Off.

6 So That's What Crying Sounds Like

Confession: I never knew my house was so noisy.

The water faucet sounded like Niagara Falls while the kitchen stove vent blasted like Hurricane Groves. My son's once teeny-tiny voice became a Lion King's roar. "No want to go potty! No want to take nap! Stop, Mommy! Stop!" Nicklaus' words cut through to the center of my nerves. With my hearing aids on, the world was deafening, if that were even possible for a hard-of-hearing person. Even Ron, who had once been impossible to lip read because of his mumbled speech, seemed to shout at me.

With no volume control on my new set of ears, I resigned myself to putting up with the full-wattage noise as long as it didn't produce a migraine.

It didn't help my stress level that Ron and I were trying to get pregnant. Wasn't I supposed to be relaxing and glowing in my impending maternal bliss? My whole body was a ball of nerves.

"Ah! Mommy! Ah!"

I heard Nicklaus' piercing cries from my bedroom. I had just turned the shower head off and, without my hearing aids on, the only noise I heard in the quiet bathroom was the shrill wailing of my toddler son.

With a towel wrapped around me, I sprinted to the bedroom. Nicklaus stood with his back to me, facing the room's enormous window. Great, now neighbors were gonna get an eyeful of a dripping wet momma in her scanty towel.

Then I saw it. Nicklaus' hand was stuck in the window sill. His left ring finger was stuck beneath the window.

"Mommy! Ahhhhh!"

I wrapped my arms around his torso, trying to free him from the window trap. He wouldn't budge.

With one hand holding onto him and another on the window, I pushed up on the glass. It raised just enough to free his hand and for me to see what was left of his finger.

Resting in the window sill was the pearly white fingertip of my little boy's left ring finger. Blood oozed out of his decapitated finger. I used my towel to catch the falling drops as I whisked him away to the bathroom sink.

I drenched his hand in cold running water while the sink filled with his scarlet blood.

While he cried, I tried to figure out what caused his finger catastrophe. Nicklaus had been playing in the bedroom next door to the bathroom while I showered. I hadn't been able to hear him with the faucet head spewing and my ears ringing like they always did. My hearing aids had been in their special carrying case in my purse, far away from the shower water that would have damaged them.

My ears were to blame for Nicklaus' bloody finger. If I had showered before he woke up, I would've had my hearing aids in and been more observant. If I didn't have hearing loss, I may have been able to multi-task showering and hearing for my son in the next room. If I had been more on top of things, I would've kept him away from an open window that he somehow managed to lower onto his left ring finger.

Mommy guilt oozed through me as Nicklaus' blood dripped into the sink. What should I do? Call Ron? Sure, but since he worked dozens of miles away, what could he do? Call my mom? She lived in another state. Drive Nicklaus to the ER? How could I drive while holding him, he wouldn't get into his car seat in his fragile state?

I left Nicklaus at the running faucet, raced to the phone, and dialed 9-1-1.

"9-1-1. How may I assist you?"

"Huh?" I couldn't hear over Nicklaus' wailing. I plugged my free ear with a finger to block out the noise.

"You dialed 9-1-1. How can I help you?"

"Uh, yes. My son. He hurt his finger. At a window. It got. Chopped off. I need an. Ambulance. Please. Hurry."

After reciting my name, where I lived, and how sorry I was for taking a shower while my boy played, I hung up and prayed.

"God. I know I don't talk to you much, except when I need help, but please be with my boy. I'm so sorry. I'm so, so sorry."

The blood trickle from Nicklaus' finger eased up, and I wrapped several tissues around it then raised it to help it clot. At least I knew how to stop a finger's bleeding.

While he sat on the toilet with his tissued hand, I reached for my clothes and got dressed. I didn't even bother looking in the mirror. My shame was so apparent, I could see it without even peering at my reflection.

⁓

The ambulance pulled to the curb as I slid my feet into shoes. I grabbed my purse and held Nicklaus against my hip.

The ambulance lights flashed as a paramedic helped us step

into the van. Another paramedic marched into the house to retrieve Nicklaus' fingertip.

While the sirens blared, the paramedic propped me and Nicklaus onto a gurney. Nicklaus lay between my legs.

"It will be alright, Ms. Groves."

"Huh?" All I heard were garbled words with Nicklaus' whimpering cry and siren noise serenading us in the background.

"Your son. It will be alright."

I strained to hear this paramedic. Why was I struggling to hear him when I had my hearing aids in?

Wait. Where were my hearing aids?

My purse dangled at my shoulder, and I reached for the hearing aid carrying case inside.

I pulled an aid out then realized my hair was sopping wet from the shower. Hearing aids couldn't get wet. There was no way I could wear my hearing aids in the ambulance.

This was going to be a long, exhausting drive to the ER.

Machines beeped from inside the ambulance, which competed with the frenzy of Nicklaus' cries, a paramedic's questions, and the CB radio up front. As Nicklaus lay on my lap, I stroked his dark blond hair with my sweaty fingertips. He began to calm down, while my pulse raced inside of me. Somehow, my pulse sounded louder to my ears than all the noise from inside that medical van.

After wheeling both me and Nicklaus via gurney to the examining room, the paramedics finally stopped my boy's wailing — thanks to a stuffed animal they gave him, which Nicklaus squeezed with his uninjured hand. A plastic baggy nearby held the remains of his pencil eraser-sized fingertip.

"There is no need for surgery," announced Dr. Lab Coat upon inspecting the base of Nicklaus' finger. "His body will grow a new one."

With my hearing aids still tucked away, I attempted to lip-read the doctor's rapid-fire sentences. I was coming up short.

"Grow a new WHAT?" I asked.

"Fingertip."

"Finger WHAT?"

"Fingertip. Just keep his hand clean, dry, and bandaged. And in a month, his fingertip will grow back."

As I let the words register, I caught my reflection in the mirror above a sink across the room. My makeup-less cheeks turned pale pink in the glass. I swallowed to keep from gagging over thoughts of a bloody, severed finger coming to life again.

"We are going to need to give him a shot in the injured finger to control the pain." Dr. Lab Coat motioned to my now content boy. "You might want to hold him because it's going to hurt."

I had heard the words, but I didn't want to accept them. The doctor was going to do what? And did he say it was going to hurt?

Before I could swallow again, a nurse arrived with a sharp metal injector that she held like a torch.

Ms. Nurse with a Needle reached for Nicklaus' makeshift bandaged hand. She smiled as she unraveled the gauze.

"Hello. I like your stuffed animal," she said, easing the needle toward the cartilage between Nicklaus' left ring and middle fingers. "This will only hurt a minute."

I wrapped my arms around Nicklaus' torso. I closed my eyes and swallowed. Nicklaus' delicate body tensed as if injected with a bolt of electricity.

Then he screamed. Even without hearing aids. Even with hearing loss. Even if I had been deaf and lived on a remote island a million miles from where my son sat, I would have heard his scream. It gushed into the center of my eardrums and sprayed every nerve ending in my body.

While my child lay moaning from pain and shock, I wrapped my arms around him tighter and let the pain become mine. Mommy guilt wrapped its arms around me. Why had I let him fool around near a window while I showered? I never heard anything in the shower, except my off-key singing. How could I have trusted my messed up ears to hear him from another room?

Not only did I have lousy hearing that couldn't detect a falling window on my son's hand, but I had lousy judgment to leave a mischievous toddler by himself for twenty minutes.

I wanted to curl up in a tight ball, roll out of that emergency room, and die.

The first dream I remember having was at the age of six.

A round man wearing a sloppy white T-shirt, along with his scissor-fanged mutt dog, chased me and my friends through our small-town Oklahoma neighborhood.

"Git outta here, 'fore I sic the dog after ya," Fat Man hollered at us.

One of the ornery boys running with me hissed back, "What's you gonna do, eat us? Fat pig!"

The wind whipped at our faces, while Killer Dog snapped at my heels.

"Hurry up," I called to my friends.

No one turned to notice Killer Dog and Fat Man within arm's reach of my faded Wrangler's and worn Buster Brown loafers. When I looked at them, the man belted out, "I'mma gonna git you."

When I closed my eyes, the entire dream became black except for white bones. In front of me and behind me, skeletons hung in the air by invisible cords. More bones hung in front of me, and they were small. One set of bones wiggled and danced out of control. Just like the ornery boy before Fat Man hollered at us.

Behind me was one set of bones, and they were huge. The spindly bones where fingers should've been were curled into fists. Just like Fat Man's fists as he threatened to "git me."

Out of the darkness stood one solid object — the dog. Killer Dog's fur, ears, eyeballs, and scissor teeth shone in my face. Dangling out of the dog's mouth was one single Buster Brown loafer.

I waved my fingers in front of me. Slowly, my slender white bones faded to black.

"MOM!"

I rolled over and stared at the clock. 7:05 a.m.

"Mom, I hungry."

I yanked at the bed covers and flipped them over my head.

"Mom, want bek'fast."

I pushed fingers into each of my ears to plug them.

Nicklaus banged on his bedroom door. With a child-proof doorknob, he could only get out of his room if I opened it. In his own room, he would be safe, not free to wander the house on his own or pull windows down on his fingers.

If I didn't keep him barricaded, I couldn't sleep in. Or have recurring dreams about being a kid and running free, then facing the white bones.

I unplugged my ears and pushed the covers off my head. 7:08 a.m. I had to get up.

My mornings had become slower, grayer, more dream-filled in the last few weeks. Ever since Nicklaus lost his fingertip and grew it back again, I struggled to get out of bed.

I'd force myself awake, stumbling to the shower, hot water on my face, dripping wet hair fresh out of the shower, hearing aids immediately plugged into each clean ear. I'd wait for the tiredness to fade as I combed my hair, rubbed lotion on my bloated skin, and tried to stop the retching reflex that hit me each morning between eight and nine o'clock.

The week my period started then stopped abruptly, I'd purchased a home pregnancy kit. The white stick produced double blue lines within a minute.

I was with child, and I felt like throwing up.

7 Do Pregnant Moms Dream in Color?

Confession: I never loved my pillow more.

I saved the e-mail, unsure of whether to send it. What was I doing writing a childhood teacher I hadn't seen or talked to in twenty-five years?

Dear Ms. Carpenter,

I'm not sure if you remember me. Back in the late '70s-early '80s, you were a Sunday school teacher at Deer Creek Baptist Church. I visited there with my grandparents and parents, and when I was 8, asked Jesus into my heart and was baptized.

We all go through life wishing we had told others what a difference they made in our lives. I want you to know what a difference you made in my life when I was a child.

I remember sitting in your Sunday school class, captivated by your teaching ability. During one class, we discussed the habit of smoking and how it was very unhealthy. My parents and grandparents, at the time, smoked, and I was so ashamed and afraid of their bad habit. Would they get sick? You seemed to offer our class words of wisdom that I have never forgotten. God loves us no matter what our "filthy habits" are.

This e-mail may seem odd, but there was some reason God allowed our paths to cross, first in that sweet country church, and now via e-mail. You are an amazing teacher, and your teaching made an eternal difference in my life...

UGH! I closed the e-mail. What a crazy person I was to draft such a sappy, over-Christianized letter to a woman I hadn't seen for years — basically, a stranger.

Thoughts rolled through my brain. First, my pregnancy and whether I would be a good mother to this child. Then, my childhood.

The past seven years, my relationship with my parents had grown more strained. I didn't agree with their humble countri-fied ways, and I assumed they didn't agree with my move to the big city. I rarely visited them.

At the twenty-week ultrasound, I found out this unborn child growing in me was a girl. In fact, she would be the first female born into Ron's family in fifty-five years.

I grew up with two sisters — one older, one younger, each born three years apart. Miss-Independent-Big-Sister-Lydia and Scissor-Happy-Little-Sis-Janie. I knew a bit about girls and their emotional tendencies, since I shared a room with sisters from the time I left the hospital as a seven-pounder until the year I got my driver's license. As the middle child, I automatically gained experience as a playmate to Janie while pretending to be an adult to Lydia. I didn't want to get on Lydia's nerves, so I did what she said. I didn't want Janie to be unhappy, so I played Barbie's with her long after it was cool for a teen to do so.

Maybe all this femininity growing in my womb was re-sponsible for my current craziness. Hormonal ups and downs, wishy-washiness, letters to mere strangers, thinking about my sisters, and bizarre rantings to my unborn child.

Dear Baby Girl in my Tummy,

Do you know why I don't get along with your grandma right now? She wants me to call Lydia and apologize to her for something she misunderstood. Yes, Lydia is welcome in my home. No, Mom, Lydia does not have to get a hotel room the next time she's in town. I only told Lydia that I didn't think it was a good idea to have her over at my house because, at the time (three years ago, to be exact), I was pregnant with another baby that took all the energy out of me. What type of a hostess would I have been in my retching, sleep-all-Saturday state?

But really, it's Little-Sister-Janie who is Mom's sole focus now. Janie is the one raising two-year-old twins as a single mom. Janie is the one working crazy hours as a beautician and in need of Mom's childcare. Janie is the one who meets a guy she likes, marries him, gets bored, then moves onto the next adventure. Janie is the one who gets a tattoo in the design of a paisley stripe in the center of her stomach to show her creativity. Janie is the one who keeps your grandma and grandpa awake at nights and makes them too tired to make the five-hour drive to see me.

So, I'm a little perturbed that I have to apologize to one sister, make allowances for another sister, and take your grandma's guilt-trip-ridden phone calls. Which, by the way, I struggle to hear because I am going deaf!

Love,
Your Pregnantly Pensive Mom

My head was also spinning from crazy dreams.

I was about to deliver the baby and I was spending the night at my parents' house. All of a sudden, the contractions rippled through my abdomen, and I fell to the floor. Mom and Dad found me on their living room floor, clutching my stomach.

"It's trying to come," I cried.

Another contraction tore through my tummy. Everything inside my midsection burned, as if someone had doused my skin in kerosene and lit a match. I turned onto my side, knees curled into my chest.

"Probably something she ate." Mom took a puff from her cigarette.

Dad knelt beside me and examined my stomach. "You sure that's a baby in there? 'Cause I don't see anything."

Ouch. Each breath more painful than the next. Contractions seconds apart, in sync with every mouthful of air. The only thing that offered comfort was to roll onto my side, cup my hands beneath my baby bulge, and tense my entire body.

"Jimmy," Mom called to my dad. Her voice stopped. All I heard, besides the grinding of my teeth as I writhed in labor, was her gasp. My body may have hurt, but oddly enough, I could hear her without lip-reading.

"Oh, good gravy." Mom said his name slower now. "Jimmmmm-eeeeee."

After my contraction stopped, I felt a tickle between my legs. I patted the front of my shorts, and my hand touched what seemed to be tiny toes.

"It's comin' out," Dad said.

Mom bent over me. "Jimmmmm-eeeee. Go get some towels."

Dad raced down the hall while I curled into another contraction and closed my eyes.

Someone slid a towel under my legs and tugged on those tiny feet until I felt them slide out of me. As the baby was born, the lower half of my body numbed. I opened my eyes to find Mom stubbing out her cigarette in the coffee table ashtray.

In Dad's arms was a glistening wet baby with wavy, chocolate brown hair — a boy.

The newborn smiled at me.

I was not only pregnant with child, I was pregnant with random thoughts. While at my parents' tiny house before succumbing to labor pains in the dream, I lay in the same full-size bed from my childhood.

It was the one Janie and I had tossed and turned in as kids, fighting over covers. Some nights, we talked about boys. I remembered a conversation we had when I was about to hit puberty and Janie tried to convince me of how cool she was at the age of ten.

"Let's say the goodnight prayer," she said.

I rolled my eyes. "Whatever... Goodnight."

"Goodnight," she chimed in.

"I love you."

"I love you, too."

"Forever."

"Forever."

"No matter what we do."

"No matter what we do."

I turned on my side and pretended to snore.

Janie reached over and poked my shoulder.

"What about the boys?" she whispered.

This was the part of the prayer, which wasn't really a prayer, that annoyed me. Every TV, movie, or rock star Janie had a crush on made it into this part of the prayer.

"I love..." Janie paused. "I love... Kirk Cameron!"

Ughh! "Corey Haim."

"Corey Feldman."

"You mean, Gross Corey?" I threw my pillow over my head.

"Tom Cruise," she said.

I lay there, pretending to ignore her.

"Tom Cruuuise," Janie announced again into my pillow.

"Stupid," I mumbled.

Janie grabbed my pillow and ripped it off my head.

"Tom Cruise!" Her words sprayed spit on me.

I kicked her toes with the calloused part of my heel.

"No fair. You're not saying the goodnight prayer."

Janie yanked the covers off.

"Give 'em back." I let her have it with my heel again, this time in the small of her back.

"Hey..." She rolled over and rubbed her back. "No fair," Janie yelled, throwing the covers back in my face.

I woke up. Now a pregnant mom for the second time, I rolled out of bed and flipped on the TV news.

"Mild summer temps continue this July day," the captions

flashed at the bottom of the screen. My swollen, heat furnace of a body wanted to celebrate. No sweltering summer day for this lip-reading momma.

I had given up trying to lip-read the news anchors. My latest quest was to make sure that every television set in the house had closed captioning turned on.

Shortly into this pregnancy, my life changed when, on a whim, Ron offered to turn the subtitles on while we squeezed onto the couch to watch a DVD. Prior to that, I had dozed through half of Season One of *The Sopranos.*

"Tony," the captions blazed across the screen. "We gonna have real problems if we don't get this here situation cleaned up."

The "situation" was a rival mobster stealing business and cash from mafia king Tony Soprano's gang. I later watched in pregnancy morning sickness horror as they decapitated the rival's head.

Nicklaus waltzed into my bedroom as I rubbed lotion onto my grotesquely stretched, vein-marked abdomen.

"Wanna watch Arthur. Wanna watch Elmo." He smiled his cherubic smile.

I motioned at my unmade bed. "Hop up."

I tossed the lotion bottle aside and reached for the remote. The kiddie channels were memorized. No Arthur on this early. But Elmo would be gearing up about now.

It was 10:35 on a Monday morning, and we both were just out of bed.

"La la lala, la la lala, Elmo's World..." The captions and friendly red monster's opening song were in perfect synch.

I crawled back into bed with Nicklaus. An oversized Old Navy T-shirt stuck out like a tent over my belly button.

As the lovable Elmo sang to his goldfish, then to his pantomime friend, Mr. Noodle, I returned to my daydreams.

With enough energy to drive myself to the OB doctor, I walked to the check-in desk with Nicklaus at my scaly heels, and plopped into a waiting room chair.

Nicklaus skipped into the playroom to check out the mini-picnic table with crates of children's books, beanbag chairs, and flat screen TV. I sat glued to my chair. This pregnancy had taken my will to chase after Nicklaus. The doctor blamed my inertia on anemia. I swallowed dime-sized iron supplements each day to nourish my weakened blood.

As I closed my eyes, I listened to the waiting room music via my hearing aids. It sounded like a harp and violin rendition of The Beatles' "Let It Be," but I could've been mistaken.

"Mrs. Groves."

Was that stringed melody chanting my name? A finger poked my shoulder.

"Miss-us Groves," a woman in puke-green nurse scrubs said. "We can see you now."

I dug my fists into the chair, pushed myself up stomach first, and nearly fell onto the nurse. My back hurt something fierce, and my entire middle cramped.

"You okay?" Ms. Scrubbed-Out Nurse asked.

Before I could answer, another spasm grabbed at my back and abdomen. I waved at Nicklaus sitting on a beanie bag to come on. He quickly shot out of the playroom and down the hall, straight for the fishbowl of suckers at the nurses' station.

It was the day before my due date. My baby girl could be born anytime — as my contracted stomach brutally reminded me.

Someone else would have to chase my little boy.

8 Are You There, God? It's Me, Shanna.

Confession: I wonder if Judy Blume ever felt pain.

I felt like giving birth right there in the SUV.

Our car sped seventy-five miles an hour down the highway while Ron gripped the steering wheel, all the while encouraging me to breathe.

"You're doing great," he said as he cut off another motorist merging into our lane. "Almost there."

In between back spasms, I tried breathing deep. It wasn't working. My back, not my stomach, felt all the labor pains.

"Hee-hee-hee," I hissed, gasping for air.

Ron said he could see the hospital, but all I could see was the forest green dashboard in front of me as my mind attempted to focus on something other than death-defying back labor.

Ron sped into the hospital parking lot, then eased to a stop at the valet drop-off.

"Your keys, sir?" a smiling valet attendant said, holding his palm out to Ron's car window.

"Wipe that smirk off your face," I nearly barked.

Ron jumped out, dropped the keys in Smirk-Jerk's hand, and disappeared behind the hospital entrance doors.

Baby pains gripped at the base of my spine, ripped through my pelvis, and bore an imaginary hole into my lower abdomen.

"Hee-hee-hee."

I wanted to die. Where was Ron? I wanted him to die.

The doors opened, and out came the man who got me pregnant, pushing a wheelchair.

"Hee-hee-hee. Help!"

What could Ron possibly do to help — take on my labor? Biologically impossible. But with each back, pelvis, and abdominal spasm, I wanted to rip out my ball of pain and fling it at him. Watch him fall to his knees. Claw at the parking lot pavement. Cry to God for mercy.

The thoughts provided a few seconds of delirious comfort.

Ron opened my door and reached for my hand. "Careful."

Yeah, if we'd been careful, I wouldn't be carrying this ball of walloping baby pain.

The wheelchair waited for me like a queen's throne. If I had felt better, I would have pasted on a diva smile and shouted out for everyone in the hospital to hear: "Watch out, 'cause here comes Mad Mama on wheels!"

My limp body fell into the chair as another pain stabbed its knife into my lower back.

Once, I passed out while covering a story for a small town newspaper. My assignment was to watch a video — "What Happens to People When They Are Shot," then interview the local police department about gun safety. As images of victims' injured limbs flashed across the screen, I felt all the saliva on my tongue dry. I stood to leave after a gun-mutilated head photograph appeared.

"Ma'am, you need any help?" someone called after me as I stumbled down the hall. I was speechless, barely able to keep my feet shuffling forward. Everyone who passed me had the same horrified expression. Faces faded from color to black and white

— the tell-tale sign that my consciousness was fading. I didn't remember falling onto a chair, fainting, then peeing all over myself.

Would I pass out in my queen-for-a-day wheelchair?

"Hi, Mrs. Groves. How are you feeling today?" A cheery woman in pastel polka dot hospital scrubs smiled, gripping a medical chart. At least I think that's what she said. I had been so busy trying to keep this baby inside of me that I left home without my hearing aids.

Ron rubbed my shoulders in the reassuring way I knew too well. It was our signal when I didn't understand someone's question. He would do the listening and talking for me.

"She's been having pains for the last few hours," he said, giving my shoulders the full massage treatment. "Doctor told us to come on in."

Then Ron did something I also knew too well. He whispered something that I couldn't hear, but I knew what those words were. I had memorized them. In restaurants, at family gatherings…anyplace the people around me didn't know I was hard of hearing, Ron made a point to mouth the words, "My wife has hearing loss."

I glanced up at Miss Polka Dot Scrubs and watched her cheerful smile melt into a knowing, pinched-lip expression. "I see," her face seemed to say.

"We're going to check your blood pressure," she said with exaggerated enunciation. It was as if each word she spoke was its own sentence. I cringed at her words, while my lower spine convulsed in labor pain.

Inside the maternity ward, Polka Dot and Ron lifted my bloated body out of the wheelchair. As the blood pressure cuff tightened its death grip, Polka Dot placed a stethoscope to my chest and plugged it into her ears. She recited the blood pressure tally to Ron and gave me a thumbs up — her degrading version of sign language.

"Okay," Polka Dot belted in her theatrical voice. "Let's see how far you're dilated."

Before I could object, she whipped out rubber gloves, slid them over her hands. Her cold, clammy fingers poking around my lower body were nothing compared to the walloping contractions that flowed through my tummy. On a scale from one to ten, with ten being the worst, my pain was a fifty-five.

"Well, well. You are dilated to a six." Polka Dot spoke with Shakespearean diction. "Do you want an epidural?"

Ron leaned in close to the nurse. In a hushed voice he said, "She..."

"Just give me the shot," I snapped. Sweat beads popped above my eyebrows. My tongue was as dry as the skin on a seventy-five-year-old woman. It lay limp between my teeth, which promptly chomped down whenever a contraction struck.

Polka Dot surveyed my face. "I'll be right back."

Where was she going? I wanted to hunt down the pain shot, inject myself with its feel-good vibes, and then throw the needle in her face.

I had dreams of someday working for *The New York Times* as a Lois Lane wonder-reporter. Lois never got pregnant by Clark Kent. That would have derailed her entire fact-finding career.

"I'm so far away from Lois Lane."

Polka Dot leaned into the hospital bed where I convulsed. An anesthesiologist stood with Ron on the sidelines, watching my horrific labor.

"We're going to do the epidural now," Polka Dot said in Shakespearean fashion. "I want to show you how to lay for the anesthesiologist."

I imagined Mr. Long Needle flashing a wicked grin from behind me.

Polka Dot squeezed her fists and bent her elbows to her chest. Then, as if rehearsing for the part of Lady Macbeth, she eloquently hunched over, to expose her lower back.

"I want you to squeeze your body, like this." she said. "Like a frightened cat."

What the — meow?

"When the anesthesiologist gives the epidural, I want you to freeze this position." She locked eyes with mine, her mascaraed eyelashes touching her eyelids. Polka Dot raised her fist and gave the thumbs up. "Okay?"

Ron raced over to face me and grabbed my fists. He flashed a smile of loving support. I ground my teeth. A cold, wet alcohol swab tickled my lower part as the anesthesiologist performed his pre-cleansing epidural routine. My body froze into the cat position.

One. Two. Three.

A full-blown contraction ripped through my body as the mile-long epidural needle entered my back. I felt its stinging, icy poke.

After some more tinkering with the epidural shot and affixing a bandage, Mr. Long Needle waved goodbye. I lay on my side in agonizing labor pain, until the medicine started flowing through my back, abdomen and legs, covering me like a nice, warm blanket.

"It's working," I said to Ron. The first words I had spoken since bellowing, "Huh? What'd you say?"

Despite not having my hearing aids in and being essentially deaf, I could hear him say over and over, "You're doing great."

I felt great — for about fifteen minutes. Then a ripple of pain ran down the right side of my stomach and back.

"You're dilated to a ten," Polka Dot said. "I'll get the doctor."

As soon as she left, the right-half of my abdomen and back tensed into a ball of pain. On a scale from one to ten, the discomfort was at an eight. My left side remained numb.

"I don't think it's working," I said to Ron as I pointed to my right side. "I feel everything."

He dabbed at my forehead with a moistened hospital rag. "You're doing great. Just great."

Was I talking to a robot here?

Dr. Susie, my laid-back O.B. doctor, strolled into the room as if entering her best friend's college dorm room. She wore a surgical mask around her ears, with the front pulled down to expose her rosy pink lips and cheerleader's smile.

She kneeled at the foot of my bed with Polka Dot behind her, shining what appeared to be a surgical flashlight.

"Baby's about to crown," Dr. Susie said.

Polka Dot looked up. "T net con action," she said, "I wa poo wee haha, k?"

Huh?

Ron leaned over my face, within a few inches of my nose.

"She wants you to PUSH," he said. "Next CON ACTION."

Push when?

How could I focus on lip-reading Ron and everyone else when the entire right half of my body tightened like a helium-filled balloon?

"Tee tee poo," Polka Dot said.

Huh?

"Poo, Shanna," said Dr. Susie.

What?

Ron's voice echoed, "PUSH. PUSH!"

I closed my eyes and tried to force that baby out of me, despite experiencing the worst pain known to womankind on my right side. It felt as if a steel-toed boot was stomping at my groin.

Every person in the room — doctor, nurse, Ron — repeated the one-word instruction to push.

I clamped down on my teeth, and my entire face throbbed from the exertion of doing that one word.

Push. Push. Push.

I was running out of push power. Ron leaned in, told me I was doing great for the sixty-billionth time, and held one of my hands. My fingernails clawed into his skin.

Push.

"Ah!" I cried.

"You doo doo gee."

Push.

"Doo gee."

My ears, which normally rang like whistles and bells every hour of the day, now sounded as if a thousand steam engines were blaring inside them. I couldn't hear my voice.

Poo.

Huh?

POO!

I gritted my teeth hard like knives. I pushed that baby out of me like it was a trapped bird attempting to escape its locked cage.

The next sound I heard, besides the noise of my ear trains, was a piercing baby cry.

"It's a grrr!" Polka Dot yelled.

I leaned my head back into my sweat-soaked pillow as she held the bloody baby up.

Ron leaned into my face, tears welling in his green eyes. "Goo jaaa."

I couldn't hear him that well over the steam engines. And I

couldn't stop shaking from the pushing. I couldn't stop grinding my teeth. Instead of holding this baby I had brought into the world, all I wanted to do was punch someone.

Had an imaginary rubber band in my brain just snapped?

Murdering someone seemed better than holding a baby.

9 Happy Pills

Confession: Swallowing hard stuff makes me gag.

I held the tattered leather Bible, which I had nearly forgotten about in the tangle of cobwebs under my bed. This was the Bible Mom bought for me when I was in high school — such a vague memory now. I couldn't remember the last time I had opened it.

Exhausted from another sleepless night, I opened the book to clear my thoughts and maybe even inspire myself.

"So much for that," I said after reading a proverb. I tossed the Bible on the floor.

The house was silent as I coerced my body out of bed. Ron had left for work at dawn, and Nicklaus and our new daughter, Reagan were sleeping in. It was only me, and my legs that felt like lead.

My engorged breasts desperately needed the milk to be released. Reagan slept yet another night without waking up to be fed. The first time she did this, I thought she had died in her sleep. Three months later I was still waking up before she did.

My swollen body ached for a shower, so I lumbered to the bathroom and turned the water on. When the temperature was warm enough, I pulled off my nightshirt and stepped in.

The water sprayed my hair, shoulders, and down my body.

As it pelted my skin, the circulation slowly returned to my legs.

What are you doing, Shanna?

This thought caught me off guard as I applied a steady stream of soap to my calves. I expected to hear this inner voice at night-time during my restless, dreamless sleep. But not this early.

You expect a shower to clean off the grime?

I grabbed my razor, pretending not to hear the voice. I pulled the razor up my lathered legs, removing the stubble that had grown overnight. Easy stroke upward, then clean the razor with water. Repeat.

It's not that simple. You can't shave the dirt away.

"Ouch!"

I tossed the razor as a line of blood trickled from a cut on my ankle, down my foot and onto the shower floor. Soap from the top of my legs slid down to my ankle, reaching the bloody spot. The white and the red mixed together and formed a pink liquid that emptied into the drain.

You can't shave it away. Your problem is still there.

"Stop it!" I screamed. "Leave me alone."

Since Reagan's birth, the accusing voice had become my constant companion. Three months later, it still filled my thoughts.

I picked up the razor.

You know what razors do, Shanna.

I eased the razor back up my lower leg, careful to avoid the bloody, gaping cut.

Razors don't clean. They kill.

My fingers locked onto the razor in a fierce grip. There was still one leg left to shave while the other one bled.

You see, Shanna. You can't make it stop. The bleeding, it's not going to stop. You can't make it stop.

I pretended the voice didn't exist. It was only me and the razor. The sharp blade slid up my leg in one swift motion. I was oblivious to the fact that if I wasn't careful, I could accidentally cut myself again.

You can't make it stop. You are only heading in the same direction as those before you.

Fierce stroke upward. Repeat. Scrape, scrape.

Your mind is only meant for hearing voices. Just like your dead uncle. Just like your wacko grandmother. Just like her syphilitic father.

Red and white mixed together. Pink liquid. Scrape, scrape!

You can't stop it. Even Janie, your own sister, hears voices. They tell her to abandon her children, steal from your parents, and buy pills that will poison her body. Over and over again.

Fierce stroke, repeat. Water. Red. Wet. White foam. Pink. SCRAPE!

You can't stop it because you're just like all of them. You tried to get married to a normal guy. Then you moved away from your family. You confronted your mother, then wouldn't speak to her for two months. You hoped becoming a mother and holding babies in your arms would keep you grounded. You'd be different than how your grandmother had been with her children. But just wait. Your children are going to resent you.

I tried to hold the razor, but my fingers shook.

"Whoever, whatever you are," I yelled. "Just stop it!"

I put down the razor, rinsed what was left of the blood and soap from my leg, and turned off the shower.

I grabbed a towel from a nearby rack and wrapped it around my body before stepping out onto a soft rug. The cool bathroom air surrounded around me.

I reached for a piece of toilet paper to clean off the blood, then discarded the soiled paper into the trash can. The wound would need a bandage.

I sat on a bench next to my vanity and reached into the cabinet, grabbed a box of small bandages and unwrapped one, taping it to my ankle.

The mirror reflected my wet, matted blonde hair. My eyes, which were normally an azure color, were now an overcast blue from lack of sleep.

Ron considered it a blessing we had a baby who could sleep so soundly at night. The first night Reagan rested so peacefully in her crib, Ron patted me on the back and said, "Well, Shanna. It looks like you'll be getting a lot of sleep, too." That night, I lay in bed a long time, my stubborn body refusing to relax. I couldn't sleep, couldn't dream — although I tried. I could only lie there while a voice spoke brutal thoughts to me. In the months since Reagan's birth, the voice spoke to me again and again.

What are you doing, Shanna? What are you doing?

"Mommy, what are you doing?"

Nicklaus stood there holding his favorite stuffed animal, a lamb. He wore a short-sleeve pajama shirt with matching pants that snapped at the waist.

"Who were you talking to?" he asked, rubbing his eyes.

My shouting in the shower must have woken him.

"Momma got hurt," I said. "I was just saying 'ouch.'"

"What did you hurt?" Nicklaus asked, sitting beside me. The stuffed lamb was nearly half his height, but somehow he managed to fit it in his lap.

I pointed to the bandaged ankle.

Nicklaus wrapped his arms around the lamb. "Why were you sad last night?" he asked.

I picked up a comb and began working it through my

tangled hair. I really wasn't in the mood for a game of twenty questions, but his last inquiry did catch my attention.

"Last night? What are you talking about?" I asked, trying to untangle my hair.

Nicklaus stroked the furry toy with his hand. "You gave me a bath and got sad," he said. "Why did Daddy come in and tell you to leave?"

I thought back to how his bathwater was too cold, then too hot. I had a splitting headache as I kneeled next to his bathtub. Reagan fussed in her crib because she needed to be fed, but I was too busy.

I stopped combing and looked at Nicklaus.

"Momma was just tired, that's all."

"But, why did Daddy say go to your room?"

I picked the comb up and resumed detangling, my scalp feeling tender as I stroked it. Nicklaus stared at me while I weaved the comb in and out of my hair.

"Well," I offered, "Momma was tired. And I went to my room to rest. But my eyes were so tired, I couldn't fall asleep."

Nicklaus furrowed his brow as if he didn't understand.

"Anyway," I said, with a more upbeat tone, "I'm better now."

I glanced into the mirror and realized most of the tangles in my hair were now gone. The comb eased through another knot.

"We've got a big day planned today," I said, changing the subject. "We're putting up the Christmas tree and decorating it. I'll need your help putting the lights on."

Nicklaus met my eyes in the mirror and started to grin.

"Will there be lots of lights?" he asked, jumping up from the bench, holding his lamb.

As he stood, I managed to untangle the last knot in my hair. "Yes," I said. "There will be lots of them."

Ron set up the artificial tree that evening. Its seven-foot height seemed barbaric without the clear lights and holiday decorations to soften it.

I pulled a strand of lights from the dilapidated ornament box and plugged it in to ensure all the bulbs were working. Half of the strand lit up.

"Uh-oh," I said to Nicklaus, who was watching me while Reagan lay in her baby swing. "Better see which bulb isn't working."

I ran my hand down the portion of the cord that hadn't lit up.

"There it is," I said to Nicklaus, attempting to unscrew the burned-out bulb and replace it with a new one.

"Can I help, Momma?" he asked, his eyes blinking at me anxiously.

"Just a minute." I tried to put the new bulb in. When I was successful, the whole strand of lights flickered then they all went dark.

"What happened?" Nicklaus touched the cord, which refused to light up again.

I unplugged the lights and waited a couple of seconds before putting the strand back in the electrical outlet. The lights were still not working.

"Well, that's just great," I said, tossing aside the entire strand in frustration. "We buy new lights every year only to have them quit working."

I scrounged around in the box for another strand. My hand found one bound with a few knots. I plugged it in, and the lights flickered — a fourth of the strand went dark.

"Why is it not working?" Nicklaus asked, noticing my frustration.

I tuned him out and began wrapping the malfunctioning strand around the base of the tree.

Can't even decorate your tree, Shanna! Your grandmother threw fits if her Christmas tree didn't look perfect. Go on. Throw a fit, too.

I ignored the voice, pretending the knot in the cord and burned out bulbs didn't exist.

"Why are you doing that, Momma?" Nicklaus asked as I finished weaving the strand along the bottom of the tree and began working my way up.

Reagan started to fuss in her swing. It was probably time for her to breastfeed again.

Go on, Shanna. Throw your fit.

"Ugh!" I grunted. The strand's knot refused to wrap around the tree. Reagan's fussing grew louder and Nicklaus pummeled me with questions while I struggled to get the knot around the tree. It wouldn't budge.

I dropped the strand and reached for more lights.

"These had better work," I said as I wound the lights around the tree's lower branches. I didn't bother to plug them in to see if all the bulbs worked, but furiously wrapped them around branches, higher and higher until they scaled half-way up the tree.

I grabbed another set and twisted them around the tree. By now, it was covered with broken lights and strands not yet plugged in. The bottom half had twice as many bulbs as the top half. It was a pitiful sight.

Go ahead, throw a fit.

"Ugh!!!"

My scream matched Reagan's wailing. Nicklaus jumped. Ron's footsteps pounded down the hall.

"What's going on in here?" he asked as he walked in the room. He glanced at the tree's haphazard lights, then his eyes fixed on Reagan in the swing, her fingers curled into fists and her round face a bright pink from her wailing.

"What are you doing, Shanna?" Ron asked as I continued to search for light strands, oblivious to the alarm in his voice.

"I've gotta keep decorating," I said, my back turned. "Gotta' get more lights up."

I grabbed another strand of lights.

"Shanna, just stop!" he snapped, stomping a foot for emphasis. "Nicklaus and I will finish. Go upstairs and lie down."

Ron pointed to the stairway. "Go upstairs NOW," he repeated.

My fingers shook as I released the strand. I didn't know what to say. Instead, I headed toward the stairs.

"Why's Mommy sad?" Nicklaus asked Ron, who was gently pulling Reagan out of the swing.

I ignored my leaden legs and climbed the stairs two at a time. If I couldn't think clearly to put lights on a tree, then I needed to take a nap. Yes, that's what I needed to do.

As my stiff body fell into bed, I closed my eyes. I made my eyes stay closed. I forced my body to lie still, refusing to think about anything but the feel of the mattress cradling my head, back and legs.

~

That evening was a blur — the kids' baths, Nicklaus' story time, Reagan's breastfeeding — the usual routine came and went without a major incident. I wouldn't let myself crack. I forced myself not to get frustrated when Nicklaus shrieked over cold bathwater. I kept a stiff upper lip when Reagan resisted my breast milk.

After the children were tucked in their beds, I joined

Ron in the living room. He sat in an oversized chair, his legs propped up onto a cushy ottoman, a TV news anchor droning on in the background about the city's latest tax hike.

Ron remained quiet. I walked toward his chair and sat on the floor beside him. He was angry.

"Hon," I struggled for the right words. "I'm sorry about earlier." His eyes stayed glued to the TV.

"I don't know what happened," I said, hoping he wouldn't give me the silent treatment all night. "I've just been so...tired lately."

"And I haven't?" Ron asked. He reached for the remote control to lower the television's volume.

"I know you've been...tired, too." I forced the words out, although I had no clue he had been tired. I hadn't noticed much of anything in the last few weeks, except the sleepless nights, the leaden legs, and the harsh inner voice that continued to haunt me.

Way to go, Shanna! Some wife you are.

"You don't think it worries me," Ron said, "that when I come home from work, the kids are upset because of how you've been acting."

He looked at me. His furrowed eyebrows emphasized that he was serious.

Some mother you are, Shanna!

"And how do I explain to our son when he continues to ask me why you are upset, when I have no idea why you are?"

"You know," I said in a strained voice, "that I'd never do anything to hurt our kids. Ever."

You are such a failure! Your whole family is miserable because of you, Shanna.

Ron turned back to the TV, an exhausted look replacing the anger.

You're a failure, Shanna. A failure!

Oh, that voice! That poisonous inner voice that wouldn't go away. Before I knew what was happening, my hands flew up to either side of my head. Back and forth they went, almost beyond my control. First, they hit my cheeks, then my forehead, hair and crown of my head. Then it started all over again. I slapped the sides of my head, the front, the back. I swung my hands over and over.

Then, as if the brutal voice hadn't inhabited enough of me, it filled my throat. Its venomous words flew out of my mouth. "I hate myself!" I screamed while my hands continued to beat my head. "I hate myself! I hate myself!"

Ron couldn't watch me. He kept his eyes on the TV. He waited for my hands to stop before saying anything. Then, with his eyes glazed over, he spoke in firm, staccato sentences.

"You need help. You need to talk to a doctor. I want you to talk to a doctor. Tomorrow."

It's not like I set out to be this miserable. As I lay in bed, Ron's words reverberated. "You need help. You need help." It was like listening to a gong beating over and over.

I tossed and turned, the sheets sweaty from the exertion as I twisted them. The bed's blanket only covered my toes because I had thrown it off, its added warmth was not welcome on my perspiring body.

It wasn't supposed to be like this. Not for me at least. I remember the first time I noticed my Grandma Jean had problems with her brain. My sisters and I had spent a week one summer at her white mobile home when I was seven. One morning, Nammaw Jean whipped up a breakfast of French toast caked in egg white and covered with Karo syrup. She said Papa Larry forgot to pick up maple syrup at the store but that this syrup with a clear color had a similar taste. So all of us ate the French toast drenched in the clear sugary syrup. We ate quickly because later that morning Nammaw Jean was dropping us off at Vacation Bible School (VBS) at the Baptist church down the road.

Later at the church, after we filed into the fellowship hall and ate vanilla wafers with punch that stained our lips purple, we were led into a sanctuary for music time.

There were hymnals with musical notes printed below words that I couldn't read very well, so I memorized the songs as I heard them, "Blessed assurance, Jesus is mine," and "At the old rugged cross, where I first saw the light." Nammaw Jean had curled my hair in pink sponge rollers the night before and forcefully brushed the strands that morning. The curls were so feather soft, I thought they could fly. As I sang those songs from memory, I felt like I could fly. That if I reached my arms out and kept singing those beautiful songs, I might soar really high.

Then the singing was over and we filed out to the parking lot to catch our rides home. Nammaw Jean sat in her dark orange Chevy with the two long doors and beckoned us to get in. As she maneuvered the car out of the parking lot and onto a gravel road, she told us to pay close attention to the songs we sang in church.

She grabbed a cigarette and jammed it between her lips with one hand still on the steering wheel as she told us if we sang the songs like we meant them, Jesus would save our souls.

I was delighted. If those church songs could actually help save me, I would never stop singing them.

When it was time to get ready for VBS the next morning, I made a quick pit stop in the bathroom.

As soon as I stepped in the bathroom, I knew something was wrong. Nammaw Jean sat in the bathtub with something in her hand with a red, squishy bulb on the end. Nammaw Jean placed it between her legs and squeezed the bulb. I tried to look away, but I couldn't. Nammaw Jean saw me staring, but didn't seem to mind. In fact, she smiled and told me not to worry — this was how she cleaned the inside of her body.

I wanted to throw up. And I decided right then, I never wanted to be like Nammaw Jean.

Now as I lay curled up in the fetal position in my bed next to Ron, I realized while I was no longer seven years old, I was a grown woman with a very strong burning sensation in my stomach. I was a mother who couldn't hold her baby daughter without my insides twisting into a knot and the poisonous voice taking over my thoughts.

You're just like your grandmother, Shanna! Look what she did to your mother and your uncles, Gary and Roger. One is dead, and the other two are living with their own pain. Your Nammaw Jean damaged their souls.

I hadn't always heard this voice. I hadn't always been miserable. A long time ago I had been a joyful little girl who my mother and everyone else called Diggy. But a phone call with my mother changed that.

Two years after my wedding, I told Mom not to call me again. We spent weeks not talking to each other. I couldn't get over the fact that Nammaw Jean was crazy and couldn't forgive Mom for making excuses for her. I vowed to put my crazy, mixed-up family behind. The small handful of photos I had collected went into a shoebox, which I stuffed in a closet. My painful memories would be safe there.

Eventually, Mom and I began talking again. I don't know why

I called her, maybe because I knew she wouldn't make the first move. We tried to muster up some casual conversation, stumbling through the call — offering contrived pleasantries like, "How have you been?" and "So, how is the weather up your way?"

It would be our vernacular for years.

When Reagan was born, my thoughts started to change as I saw this child staring back at me. Her eyes were as intensely blue as mine, so wide with curiosity that a crease had already formed below her lower lashes. It was like holding a mirror and looking at a newborn version of me.

The joy should have returned, the smile on my lips should have been there, but I was wracked with conflicted emotions. My own mother and I were barely talking. Is this how it would end up with Reagan?

My daughter, with her innocence and purity, unleashed an array of emotions I had never experienced. The ominous voice in my head and its piercing words were a daily companion. As I lie awake at night, as I showered, as I fed the children and took care of them, as I made love with my husband, the voice would not rest.

For years, I had pretended to be something I was not, the poisonous voice reminded me, as I turned in my sleep. I hated what I had become. Lying beside Ron in bed, it was all I could do not to open the bedroom window, stretch out my arms, and leap out into a free fall. Would the voice be silent then?

Still lying awake with my husband's arm around my waist, I gently rolled over onto my side and felt underneath the bed. My fingers finally touched the tattered edges of a leather book. I grabbed it and pulled it onto my lap. I couldn't open my Bible, but I knew I needed to hold it. The book I had tossed aside that morning, I now clung to. I held it tightly to my chest and wept.

I couldn't admit the anguish I felt at realizing I was becoming just like Nammaw Jean. I couldn't admit the guilt I felt at turning my back on my family all those years before. All I could do was embrace the old book, my tears falling onto its leather cover and dripping off the edges.

Finally, I found the words I so desperately wanted to say. I spoke them in a hushed voice so as not to wake Ron or the kids. It was my voice, and it came from a place deep inside me.

"Help me," I prayed. "Oh, God, help me."

I sat on the padded table, Reagan propped on my knee. The appointment was for my daughter. Our family doctor was about to bring the nurses in to give Reagan her polio, diphtheria and influenza shots. I shuddered at the thought. Medicine had always intimidated me. The sight of a simple syringe made my arms and legs tense...my stomach constricting until I nearly blacked out.

"The nurses will be in shortly." The doctor, a woman in her forties wearing a white jacket over a dark-printed dress, held a clipboard with Reagan's vital statistics written on it.

"Before I go," she said, looking at me, "is there anything you need to discuss, about her diet or sleep patterns?"

Four-month-old Reagan sucked on my index finger, leaning her head over my forearm, her body not quite strong enough to sit up on its own.

"No," I replied, "everything's fine with her."

I heard Ron's reprimand in my head. "You need help. You need to talk to the doctor."

While I held Reagan, the other voice — the one that kept

me awake all hours of the night, the voice that haunted me during the day — shrieked.

Yes, Shanna, you do need help but no doctor can help you! Your grandmother tried this route, and look where it got her — living in a nursing home apartment where she stares at a TV all day.

The doctor stood up to leave. "So everything is fine then," she prodded, turning to jot down a note on Reagan's chart. Any minute, she would be walking out the door, handing the chart to a couple of nurses waiting on the other side.

What was I doing? Why couldn't I speak? Why couldn't I tell her that everything was not fine with me?

"Um, actually," I stammered. "Well...It seems that, um, I may be...depressed."

The doctor lowered her eyelids. "I'll be right back," she said, stepping out into the hall.

The room was quiet. All I could hear was the sound of Reagan sucking my finger. Where had the doctor gone?

Finally, the doctor returned with a little white box. Inside were foil-lined packages with colorful photos of middle-aged people. They were laughing and smiling, their arms draped around each other's shoulders.

The doctor took out one of the packages.

"It's very common," she said looking at me, her voice oddly sympathetic. "You are a new mom, it's winter time, and your body is going through a lot of hormonal changes."

The doctor kept talking, but I couldn't quite make out what she was saying. Reagan's sucking was getting more fierce by the minute. Finally, she released her grip from my finger, twisted and turned her body, trying to free herself from my grasp.

With each movement, she grunted, blending with the doctor's voice and filling the room with noise.

"What you have," the doctor said, "is commonly called..."

Grunt!

"...baby blues. It's really very common. I'd like you to take this package..."

Grunt, grunt!

"...and read the information on the back. These antidepressant pills are a low dose. I think they will help you get through the..."

Upset grunt!

"...winter months. I'd like you to stay on them at least through April and longer, if you would like. You should notice yourself starting to feel..."

Grunt. Twist. WAIL!

"...better within two to four weeks. Be sure to take one every day. Do you have any questions?"

I sat there stunned. The noise reverberating off the cold, white walls. Reagan wrestled in my arms, and I had just been given pills to take once a day for the next few months. And the doctor wanted to know if I had any questions?

While I continued to struggle with Reagan, the doctor pulled a second chart with sheets containing all of my health information. Surely she would notice from the sheets that I reluctantly disclosed having a family history of mental illness.

"Um, doctor," I stuttered, holding Reagan firm to assuage her fussing. "Well. Um. I'm really not sure if I want to take... Umm...well, okay."

Before I knew it, I had agreed to take the tiny white pills with "10" printed on them, enclosed in a shiny foil lining with happy people printed on the package.

The doctor nodded slowly. With her eyelids lowered once again, she told me to call with any questions. Then she excused herself from the room.

I stood up, carefully holding Reagan. My feet swayed back and forth in a rocking motion that I hoped would calm her down. But really, we both needed to calm down. We rocked back and forth, waiting for the nurses with the syringes.

~

Reagan fell asleep on the drive home. As I walked in the door, I set her baby carrier down on the kitchen floor and looked at the package of pills. The happy people on the front seemed to gawk at me as I filled a glass with water.

I pushed through the clear plastic bottom of the package, and one of the pills tore through the foil. I placed the numbered pill on my tongue, tilted my head back, and took a long drink of water. The pill felt chalky against my tongue.

What are you doing? Your problems can't be fixed by some pill.

My thoughts had to focus on something besides the pills and pain. I grabbed a package of pre-cooked meat from the fridge and waited for the poisonous voice to mock me. I waited for my brain to reel with pangs of anxiety, for my temples to throb in the beginning stages of a migraine. I waited for the hissing sound within me, the signal that the voice was about to offer its slippery accusations and threats.

I took a deep breath, holding it as I set the meat on a baking pan, opened the oven door and struggled to put the pan inside.

Come on, voice. Just get it over with.

Two small feet clomped into the kitchen.

"Mommy," Nicklaus innocently looked up at me. "Can I help?"

I released the bottled-up air and closed the oven door.

"Well..." I said slowly. Can you help me? Is there really any help for me? I focused on Nicklaus, hoping my words wouldn't

91

sputter out like a balloon losing its air.

"Well," I repeated. "There are some dishes. You could wash them." I pointed to the lunch plates I neglected earlier. "How about I fill the sink with soap and water and you help me wash?"

He nodded, elated I was letting him help in the kitchen. He hurried into the living room, returning a short time later with his little chair. He plunked it down next to the two-sided sink then climbed up, waiting for me to turn on the water.

I adjusted the faucet so the water wouldn't be too hot or too cold. "Just let me add the soap and you can get started."

As the water flowed into the sink's left drain, it pushed itself back up through the right side, now a murky gray. The more water that went down the left side, the more it pushed itself back up on the right.

"What's wrong with the sink, Mom?"

I turned the water off. There was no way I could wash dishes, finish dinner, or do anything with the sink until it was fixed. How had this happened?

My stomach constricted as I took a big breath, holding it, unable to release it. I waited for the poisonous voice to tell me I had messed everything up — that Ron would come home and have to deal with this problem I created.

Nothing. Absolute silence.

Surely I was dreaming. Either the number ten pill worked fast or my prayers were answered. I waited for the hissing sound — for the signal my head would explode and my life was about to end. It had to be a cruel joke. The voice was keeping silent until just the right moment, then it would dig its claws in and attack. It was a sick game the voice could play, like a seething Monty Hall making me a deal on door number one, only to open it to reveal a haggard goat gnawing on grass. That would be my prize. Wouldn't it?

Nothing. Absolute silence.

Unable to come up with a solution, I motioned for Nicklaus to hop off his chair and step away from the sink. I also backed away and exhaled.

The sink was broken, but it could be fixed. Maybe I couldn't fix it, but somehow it would get fixed.

I inhaled and heard a sound inside my mind. It wasn't a hissing sound. It wasn't wailing or screeching. It wasn't coming from the poisonous voice at all. It was far off, but it got louder, each time it repeated. The voice spoke again and again in a tender tone.

Who was it? Was it God? As it spoke, I felt its arms around me as it repeated melodic words, poetry intended just for me. I closed my eyes.

It will be fine, Shanna. It will be fine.

I lay motionless next to Ron, who let out a faint snore. The sound of his steady breathing blended with the gentle roar of a far-off train. The soothing ambiance beckoned sleep, but my eyes were not quite ready to call it a day.

I still felt tension in my shoulders, even with two weeks' worth of antidepressant pills now in my system. But the conflicted feeling in the core of my brain had diminished the first day I swallowed the medicine, as if the drug had instantly vanquished the poisonous voice that so long haunted me. Still, I kept waiting for the pills to make the shoulder tension go away so I could sleep.

I lay unmoving under the covers and thought about the next day. How the autumn sun would filter through the room's vertical blinds, casting streaks of light across my face. How the morning shower would pry open my eyes with their ever-present dark circles. How a plush towel would embrace my wet skin and how the sweater and pants I had neatly laid out to wear would glide effortlessly over my clean body. There would be the sound of babbling coming from the kids' rooms as they stretched, yawned and entertained themselves with peek-a-boo games under the blanket before I went in to get them dressed.

But for now, there was only white noise. The sound of my husband's breath, the soothing whistle of the train, the throbbing of my stubborn body that ached to fall into a deep sleep, where I might concoct a painting of dreamed images.

The ebony sky bleeds through the lacy drapes in my bedroom, decorated with its pink daisy quilt and an assortment of richly clad dolls. I am back at my childhood home, and my family is busy with their nightly routines. Mom is washing dishes, Dad is shaving. My sisters, Lydia and Janie, and I are in our pajamas, pulling back the bedcovers.

I glide through the routine as if I am an angel floating in a heavenly place. My heart beating steady as a drum. The cotton nightgown feels like a satin sheath, the covers as warm as vapor coming out of an oven. I wrap my arms around myself and breathe in the room's baby powder scent, the smell of my mother's cigarettes coming from the kitchen down the hall.

As I lay my head against the pillow, I hear a click, followed by a piercing pain from my head to my stomach that sends my body into spasms. I feel out of control. My mind, my arms, my legs, my words. I am overwhelmed by a heightened frenzy of movement.

Anything my flailing hands touch is grabbed and thrown against the wall. The dolls in my room become baseballs that I hurl against the door. They crack my bedroom mirror, which shatters into a startling number of pieces, distorting my reflection.

My sisters run into the room, followed by Dad. "What's going on in here?" he demands, his face bathed in shaving cream and a dripping razor in his hand.

Mom runs in, carrying the dish towel she uses to blot her soapy hands. "What are you doing, Shanna?" Her voice shaking with caution. "What are you doing?"

I run past them, barking streams of obscenities as I dart out the front door into the frigid November air. The wind whips at my nightgown and shoeless feet like an ice-cold shower, but I don't care. I leap off the front porch landing on the dormant grass, and then take off down our red-dirt driveway toward the gravel road.

The path's jagged rocks cut into my feet, but I feel no pain. I am still roaring venom at an invisible audience, and flailing my pale pink hands at imaginary ghosts.

The road leads to what looks like a gray home on top of a steep hill. As I move closer, the house becomes illuminated in an amber glow, then soft cream then, as I step on the porch, it transforms into stark white — the color of paper.

I knock on the door, my frigid body still wrestling with the inner force. The door is opened by a middle-aged woman, not much older than my mother. Her coffee-tinted hair is also similar to Mom's, but her smile is different. This woman isn't afraid to show her teeth, as crisp white as her home — her dainty arms motion for me to come in.

As soon as I enter, my upset body stills — the screech-

ing stops, my arms become as limp as falling leaves.

I become completely aware of who I am — Shanna Groves, the mother of two children, wife, sister of Lydia and Janie, daughter of Jimmy and Linda.

A young girl, who appears to be the woman's daughter and about the age of nine, stands next to a dinner table prepared with white china, linens and ceramic bowls filled with festive foods. Is this a party...some kind of holiday?

The girl invites me to take a place at the table, and I unquestionably follow her lead. As the woman and young girl are about to sit, a knock echoes at the front door. The woman walks to the door, as if she is excited to welcome another guest.

The door opens, revealing a man carrying a flashlight. Like a shadow, he stands with the opaque night sky above him.

Without warning, my body resumes the fit — my legs kicking, arms slapping out, my head violently shaking.

"Come with me, Shanna." The man reaches out and waits for me to respond. The woman and girl gaze at me with quiet eyes as if they understand my inner struggle and want so desperately to help me.

"Go ahead," the dark-haired woman says to me in a somber voice. "Take his hand."

The girl steps from the table and joins her mother next to the door, next to the man. "I want to take you to a place," the man says, lowering the flashlight to his hip. "You will find rest there, you will be safe."

"HA!" I yell in a calloused, vengeful voice as I pace the room, flailing my hands. My mind runs rampant like a vicious animal about to attack. Thoughts become

words, then streams of staccato sentences that spew out like demon-possessed shrieks.

"Go away," I growl at the defenseless man. "Go away you crazy monster! Go away!"

The coffee-haired woman places her hands on my shrunken shoulders. Her fingers feel like the dinner table's delicate fresh linen, her touch as savory as the fragrant meal. The balls of tension in my back melt at her medicinal touch.

The innocent girl, who stands waist tall beside her mother, reaches toward the open door where the mysterious man awaits. My body stills as the girl looks up at me with her slight pug nose, a gleam in her chestnut eyes. "Don't be afraid," she says through a big smile and beaming teeth. "You should go with him."

The solitary man with the flashlight has eyes of a deep chocolate brown, the same color of a worn-down man I last remember sitting in his decrepit, high-rise apartment. The old man's body had been broken down at a young age, and I, as a nine-year-old girl, never knew why. This man is someone else's father; his child was a woman I came to despise because she was a crazy, messed up, sick person — a lunatic, a psychotic woman with wads of hundred dollars bills tucked in the ripped pockets of her designer jackets. A person I called Nammaw Jean.

This man standing in the shadows is her father.

I take his hand and his blistered fingertips lace with mine. I turn to the woman and her daughter, and feel compelled to wave good-bye. Good-bye to their dinner table with its regal adornment. Good-bye to their stark white home.

I walk with the man on the narrow path leading to his car. In the black air, the car seems nonexistent even though I know it is there. He opens the door for me. I climb in on the vehicle's tattered leather seats, which scratch my legs like a bristle pad. He gets in on the other side, places one hand on the steering wheel and gazes at me. I notice his eyes. They are murky, but not sinister. Instead, they glisten with tears I can see behind his wire-rimmed eyeglasses.

"Well," he says in a barely audible voice. "You think you can trust me now?"

Before I can respond, he pulls a lone key out of his pants pocket and pokes it into the ignition. A wave of comfort washes through my pajama-clad body, flowing through my bare, blistered feet and oozing into my weary legs and stomach. It continues to my pounding chest and shoulders, finally entering my head.

Then the night sky suddenly transforms itself from a foreboding black into a sparkling glow cast from a blazing sun. The eastern sky gradually sucks away all the dark air.

I stare wide-eyed at my great-grandfather. He is not a bald old man with a sickly body and wilted posture as I remember him. He is a man in his early twenties with hair as soft and thick as down feathers, his cream skin exposing a flawless smile that spreads from cheek to cheek. He is wearing navy blue, pin-striped pants and a button-down jacket, both pressed to perfection. His polished leather shoes sparkle with spit-shine newness.

The man steers the antiquated car onto the gravel road and down the steep hill toward my parents' home.

As we drive, I let my inner thoughts overwhelm me like an ocean. I float within its current, the waves breathing health, security and peace into my body. My thoughts become words I didn't know I could say, words buried in childhood memory, filled with blinding prejudice and debilitating fear.

I speak timidly out of emotional exhaustion.

Can I trust him now? "I will try," I tell the man.

I watch as he steers the car onto a smooth blacktop road that leads toward the horizon. I glance over my shoulder and realize this is no ordinary car, but a long vehicle able to accommodate a load of people. With an elongated compartment running from behind the front seat to the rear window, I realize this is not a limousine; it is a hearse.

A second glance reveals the outlines of people's bodies sitting upright. They appear like ghosts in darkness until the sun illuminates their skin, exposing their humanity. I see the woman from the white house and her daughter. Behind them is a man who taps an unlit cigarette against the knee of his jeans.

In the farthest spot of the hearse is a young man with a leather Bible on his lap. His willowy mustache looks as if it is overdue for a trim. From behind the facial hair, his full lips mouth the word: "TRY."

My mother and father are sitting on either side of him. Their tired skin appears soft and glowing. They hold the young man's hands as their eyes fix on me.

"Where are we going?" I ask them.

10 The Long Journey Back Home

Confession: It is hard to outrun the past.

As I swallowed the tiny, numbered pill and spoke a simple prayer each morning — "Oh God, help me" — my gray mind began to reveal colors.

I grabbed a spiral-bound notebook to write my dreams and questions.

How can I take care of my family if I am a recovering depressed mom who is slowly going deaf?

I couldn't answer that one.

Why had I dreamt of riding in a hearse with my estranged family? Where were we going?

My dreams somehow connected me with taking a long journey home. The paths were never easy. Doors opened and closed. I needed to talk with family members or avoid them. Should I speak or maintain silence?

All the paths ended in a final destination, an understanding of where I had come from, where I was going. The pages filled as I transcribed all the visions that appeared in my sleep and recorded the details of my real life.

Nicklaus and Reagan napped in their rooms, and Ron was at work, so I had uninterrupted time to record these musings.

Then the phone rang.

"What are you doing?" Mom asked.

The new amplified phone was so loud, I wondered if it would wake the kids. Her voice was pleasant. We had talked a few weeks ago, and I told her I was sorry for being distant all these years. When I'd asked what I could do to make our relationship better, she told me something that stabbed at my conscience... "Accept us for who we are."

"Oh, I'm just writing away," I answered into the phone. Mom knew I liked to write in the afternoons when the house was quiet. When she and I made our peace, I admitted how much time I wasted dwelling on what she did or didn't do as a mom. I was ready to move on.

"Well now," she said.

She knew what I wrote about. We had talked about my dreams. We also discussed our family's experiences...about Nammaw Jean's mental illness, inherited from her father — the man who drove the hearse in my dream. We talked about my Uncle Gary's death of unknown causes and my sister Janie's bout with depression and drug use. And we shared our pain. Mom told me about her inner turmoil at seeing the cycle of depression continue through our family. She apologized for passing down the depression gene to me.

"I want to share something with you." Mom's pleasant voice suddenly serious.

I set my pen next to the spiral notebook and closed it.

"Sure," I said, "go ahead."

Mom paused. "You know I have been feeling so down about everything that's gone on with the family. It was really getting to me."

I ran my fingers over the notebook's smooth cover.

"Well, I was awake last night and I began to feel a peace

come over me," Mom said. "Like the Lord was with me and he was telling me He was in control of things — to not be afraid."

I tried to pay attention as I tapped my fingers on the notebook cover.

"Shanna…"

"Yeah, Mom?"

"We got a phone call today from hospice. You know they've been taking care of your Nammaw."

"What happened now?"

When Mom first told me that Nammaw had requested hospice nurses visit her at the apartment, I thought it was bogus. The only thing wrong with Nammaw, other than her bipolar disorder, was her anemia and some blood disorder that was hard to pronounce.

"I just want you to know, Shanna, that the Lord gave me the peace I have for a reason. When Hospice called today, they said your grandmother had collapsed in her apartment, and they rushed her to the hospital. The doctors said Nammaw's blood problems had taken a turn for the worse, and her circulatory system was shutting down. There isn't anything they can do for her, but give her morphine and keep her comfortable.

"Shanna," Mom said, "Nammaw is dying."

Nammaw claimed to be dying for years. Was this for real?

"What?" I said, my voice rising in disbelief. "No, that can't be right."

"The doctor sent Nammaw to a nursing home. You know, the one beside her apartment complex. There's no way she can go back to her apartment. She needs round-the-clock nursing care. She could go any time. Shanna, she's really dying."

I ran my fingers along the notebook's spiral binding, trying to absorb it all. Nammaw cried wolf so many times I didn't know whether to believe it, or laugh it off.

"She could live a few more hours, or it could be a few days. Either way," Mom said, "I just thought I would prepare you. Nammaw won't be with us much longer."

"But…what caused her circulatory system to shut down? I mean, it's so sudden. I kept thinking the hospice thing was a hoax, that Nammaw had convinced them she was dying and they actually believed her."

"It's not that simple." Mom's voice stayed calm. "Hospice began giving her morphine pills a few weeks ago. I couldn't believe it at first, but your Nammaw had been taking the morphine pills and wasn't feeling too much pain. So this morning when she stood up, her legs and feet went numb and she fell. When the hospice nurse came to check on her, Nammaw was lying on the floor, barely coherent. Apparently your grandmother really needed the morphine. She really was dying. The pills kept her from realizing how weak her body had become."

Morphine. Barely coherent. About to die. Mom presented all of this information in a few simple sentences. Had my flawed ears heard all of it correctly? As the words tossed back and forth in my head, it started to sink in.

"Oh, Mom," I said, my voice more subdued. I needed to be strong. Mom was about to lose the woman who gave birth to her, tried to raise her, and even occasionally nurtured her. She needed me. I needed to get off the phone, get in the car, and take off for Oklahoma to be with the family.

"Let me talk to Ron," I said, "but I'd like to be there. In the next day or so if I can."

"Now remember," Mom said. "She may only have a few hours left."

This could be an opportunity for me to truly make amends

with my conflicted feelings toward my family, toward the past. It was time to stop feeling ashamed, stop laughing off our family's depression history, stop pretending it didn't exist.

"I want to be there," I said.

Mom cleared her throat. "Okay. I'd better get off the phone. I'm back at the house for a while. I need to take a quick nap before heading back to the nursing home."

"Will you call me if, well..." I hesitated. The words "if Nammaw dies" hung in the back of my throat.

"Of course," Mom said before hanging up.

I sat at my desk and stared at the closed spiral notebook. The dreams I wrote about moments earlier faded in my mind. Like it or not, Nammaw Jean was a vital link to my past. In a matter of hours or days, I was about to lose that link.

I pushed the notebook aside and picked up the phone to call Ron. I had to book a trip to Oklahoma.

"Be with me now, O God. Be with me now."

I drove out of the Oklahoma City airport parking lot as I whispered the prayer. After I repeated it, I picked up my cell phone and dialed. Ron answered on the second ring.

"Good, you made it," he said. His voice echoed on the phone since I had the volume jacked way up.

"Have you heard anything from Mom or Dad, anything at all about Nammaw?" I gripped the steering wheel of my rental car.

"Nothing," Ron said.

"How are the kids?" I asked.

"They're fine."

"Good," I tried to keep focused on the road but found myself wishing Ron and the kids could have made the flight with me. I wanted to wrap my arms around Nicklaus and Reagan. When Ron suggested he stay behind while I spent alone time with Nammaw, I debated. In the end, I knew it was best this way. My feelings toward her were complicated.

The sun faded into the horizon as I promised Ron I would call him once I got settled. I continued driving as the evening sky turned dark purple and blue, like a watercolor painting. The colors slowly eased into blackness, and speckles of starlight pierced through the darkness, individually and in clusters.

I pulled off the highway onto a northbound two-lane county road that would take me to the nursing home. I traveled this road many times as a young girl in the family station wagon, Lydia and Janie wedged into the backseat with me. Although it had been awhile, the path was familiar. It was a narrow road, winding in places, straight in others — a dangerous path, that had killed a few adventurous high schoolers and oblivious drunk drivers in years past.

My stomach tightened with each pothole; fear gripped me with each turn. What would Nammaw Jean look like when I got there? Would she even recognize me?

I whispered a prayer as I pulled into the nursing home's small circle drive — a green sports utility vehicle was the only vehicle in the lot.

I stopped the car and reached for my cell phone. As I dialed Ron's number, a shadowy figure in the green car opened his door and got out. He tossed his cigarette to the ground, stepped on it and waved.

I put the cell phone in my pocket as the smiling man approached. It was my mom's brother, Roger.

I opened my door and got out as he wrapped his arms

around my back. He was wearing a brown leather jacket that matched his closely cropped hair.

"Good to see you," he said.

My chin brushed against his smooth cheek. He had spent the past two nights sitting with Nammaw Jean. I didn't expect him to have time to shave or to be so cheery.

"Is everything okay with..." I noticed his pale brown eyes appeared tired, his grin less intense than I remembered.

"Sure is," Roger said. "Boy, that grandmother of yours has a strong spirit. She's not ready to give it up yet."

"Good."

Two rows of ground-level apartments stood next to the nursing home. I had only visited Nammaw Jean's place a couple of times in all the years she lived there.

"You can stay at her apartment tonight if you like," he said, noticing my gaze. "She would want you to."

I reached in the car for my suitcase. "I think I'll stay with her in the nursing home. Give you a little break."

Roger smirked. "I probably could use a little nap."

I slammed the door shut.

"Your sister, Lydia made it in this afternoon," Roger said as we walked toward the nursing home. "She and your nephew are with Nammaw now. Think they're staying with your Mom for a couple days."

I talked with Lydia the day Mom called me about Nammaw Jean. When I told her I wasn't sure when I'd make it to Oklahoma, she warned me I would regret it if I didn't come right away.

Roger punched some numbers into the keypad at the building's double glass doors.

"You enter a special code when coming and going," Roger said as the door finally beeped. "Memorize 'em and keep them to yourself. Residents ain't supposed to know them."

I imagined Nammaw Jean waking up from her incoherent state, realizing she was trapped inside this building. No way out without the special code.

In the lobby, some of the residents sat perched in front of the lobby's large-screen TV watching a police drama. Two women sat on a couch — one wearing dress clothes and a face full of make-up, the other clutched a naked baby doll against her thick robe. A man in a short-sleeve T-shirt and flannel pants rocked his wheelchair back and forth beside the TV.

My hearing aids picked up the sound of someone yelling down the hall, "Ah! Somebody. Ah! Ah!"

"That lady sitting there with the makeup on, she looks normal, don't she?" my uncle asked. "She's in here for Alzheimer's. Pretty serious."

The stench of body odor and urine wafted through the halls. The nursing home's shiny white floors reeked of bleach. Some of the patients' room doors stood open. Most residents lay in their beds. A few sat next to small illuminated television sets.

"This is it." Roger pointed to a partially closed door with the nameplate "Una" on it.

"Who's Una?" I asked.

"Just someone who's been here a while. Your Nammaw's sharing a room with her."

He pushed the door open to reveal a dimly lit room with two twin-size beds on wheels, the area separated by a floor to ceiling drape. The only light came from a fixture above a sink and a blue glow from a TV set wheeled in on a cart.

Una lay in one bed, her eyes opening as Roger walked by. "Hello, Mrs. Peterson."

Lydia sat next to the other bed holding a frail woman's

hand. I didn't immediately recognize the person lying there. Her eyes were closed — an oxygen tube jutted out of her nose, and her mouth gaped open. Her salt and pepper gray, chin-length hair pressed flat against the bed's two pillows. The head of the mattress lay slightly elevated.

Nammaw Jean's mouth closed, then opened; her lips pale and crusty. She didn't look anything like the Nammaw I remembered, except for her long yellow fingernails that curled around Lydia's hands, when she held them.

"Where's Mom and Dad?" I asked.

"They were up here earlier. I think they went to get a snack," Lydia blotted a tear with an index finger. She gazed at me with bloodshot eyes. "Want to say hello?"

I glanced at my emaciated Nammaw lying in her bed. She had been slim most of her life, but not this thin.

"If you don't mind," Lydia said, "I think I'll head to the hotel."

"You're not staying at Mom and Dad's?"

Lydia wiped her damp hand on her pants. "I think Mom and Dad have their hands full. You know, with coping with Nammaw being sick and with Janie's problems."

She shook her head. "Can you believe our little sister? Janie came up here earlier when Mom was around and didn't even seem upset that Nammaw was dying. She was so belligerent, she had to have been high on something."

Lydia wiped away another tear. "If you stand right next to Nammaw and talk really loud, I'll bet she can hear you."

That sounded just like me and my deaf ears.

Lydia tapped Nammaw Jean's shoulder. "Hey, Nammaw. Shanna's here. She came all this way to see you."

I leaned in toward the bed and glanced at my grandmother's pasty white skin and graying hair.

When I was a girl, her hair was so dark and long, I thought she looked like a witch, especially when she wore her favorite black turtleneck. Back then, her milk white skin contrasted dramatically with her shocking dark brown hair. Her hair and skin matched each other now: colorless. My stomach tightened as I stared at Nammaw's body. She must have lost thirty pounds and shrunk three inches since I last saw her.

I grabbed a wrinkled hand. "Hello, Nammaw."

I waited for her usual "My goodness, hallelujah, it's Shanna!" greeting. Her eyebrows, once bark brown and bushy, were now transparent as she twitched them. Her lips mouthed something. Was it the word "Hello"? No sound came out.

"Hi." I swallowed hard.

Nammaw lifted her transparent eyebrows, and her eyes began to open. She turned her head toward Lydia.

"Shanna's here," Lydia said. "Flew all the way to see you."

I leaned closer so Nammaw could see my face. "I'm here."

Nammaw Jean parted her lips. Was she trying to smile or tell me something?

"It's okay," I said. "Just nod your head or raise your eyebrows if you understand what I say."

Roger patted my back. "Tell her about your kids."

"Well, uh, Nicklaus...he just started preschool," I said. "He rides a bus and really loves it. Reagan...she's getting so big. Won't be too long before she's walking all over the place."

Nammaw closed her eyes.

Lydia released her hand. "Let her rest a while."

I moved away from the bed and found an empty chair.

"Wonder what's taking Mom and Dad so long," Lydia said to herself. "I need to get checked into the hotel and can't be waiting all night for them to show up. I'm exhausted." She reached for her purse. "They need to hurry up and get here."

"Calm down," I said.

"I just don't want to be waiting all night," she said, grabbing her car keys.

Roger and I stared at the television's grainy picture. The humming of Nammaw's oxygen tank drowned out the sound. With my hearing aids in, the hum of the tank and the TV made for jarring background noise.

"I'm back." My mom's voice boomed through the din as she and my father walked in. Her puffy eyes told me she probably hadn't slept more than five hours the entire week. Her chestnut brown hair, usually parted perfectly down the middle, was brushed back away from her face, revealing three wrinkles across her forehead.

"Shanna, you made it." Mom folded her arms across her chest. "It's a good thing 'cause no one expected Nammaw to still be with us. Amazing that she is."

Lydia stood. "I've gotta go."

Mom mouthed to the rest of us, "Grouchy, ain't she?"

Nammaw Jean raised her eyebrows, her lips forming a smile. The grin was so wide her yellowed teeth and fleshy gums poked out. It grew ridiculously wide — the kind of smile people give after a photographer says "cheese."

Roger and I exchanged looks. I wondered if he thought the same thing: Would she ever smile again?

I tried not to make direct eye contact with Mom because I didn't want her to see my eyes. My lashes were wet.

Nammaw quickly went back to sleep.

Dad excused himself to go home for a nap, followed by Lydia. A hospice nurse came to take Nammaw's blood pressure and change her while Roger, Mom and I attempted to watch the static-filled TV screen.

"Why don't you sing one of those church songs?" Mom asked me. "The ones your Nammaw likes so much."

I shot my mother a look. Years ago, Nammaw Jean took me to Deer Creek Baptist Church for Vacation Bible School. It was the same church where a Sunday school teacher once told me God loves us even when we have filthy habits like smoking.

I learned dozens of songs in that church, "Softly and Tenderly, Jesus is Calling," "I Have Decided to Follow Jesus," "How Great Thou Art," "Amazing Grace" and many others.

I hummed the last song to Nammaw. Her eyebrows raised and lowered as she listened. Her lips formed an "O" shape as if she wanted to sing along.

Mom patted my arm. "She likes it."

After I had exhausted my repertoire of VBS songs, the room was quiet.

"I can stay with Nammaw a while," I finally said.

"Well, alright." Mom stood. "If you get tired, just lay next to Nammaw Jean. And be sure to call us if anything happens."

"Of course."

"I'll just be over in Nammaw's apartment," Roger said. "You'll call me if anything happens?"

I nodded.

The room's oversized wall clock read 11:25 p.m. as they walked out of the room. I got up and flipped the TV dial. The last few minutes of *The Tonight Show* played on the set's grainy screen.

My face felt flushed and sweaty. The room was too warm. As I reached for a paper towel to blot my face, I noticed a half-full cup of water with a small swab stick inside it. I knew the pink sponge tip was what hospice nurses used when giving cool water to their patients. Since many of them were unable to swallow from a cup, a nurse would soak the sponge with water and rest it on the patient's lips, moistening the chapped surface several times.

I grabbed the cup and walked toward Nammaw's bed. The last time I visited Nammaw Jean, she had greeted me with a mouthful of ice. After she opened the door and went to the kitchen sink to spit the ice out, she said this was the only way she could keep herself from smoking.

As I sat on the edge of Nammaw's metal bed with the water cup in my hand, I wondered if she craved a cigarette. How could she tell me that now? I placed the wet pink sponge on Nammaw's lips and dabbed them in small circular motions. Her lips were parted slightly, allowing me to place the swab on her tongue.

As I did this, Nammaw Jean instinctively wrapped her lips around the stick. Her tongue glided back and forth on the sponge for a couple of seconds, her eyes opening into slits.

"I'm here, Nammaw." I hoped she recognized my voice.

After her tongue released its grip on the sponge, I carefully slid it back out and placed it in the cup. Her eyelids lowered into deep sleep again.

I moved my left leg onto the firm mattress and eased part of my right leg up. There was enough room for both of us on the bed if I lay on my side, facing Nammaw.

I turned my body toward hers, trying not to disturb the sheet or blanket. Nammaw's lips had formed the "O" again, and I could hear weak breaths coming in and out of her mouth.

When I was a little girl, Nammaw Jean would wrap her arms around me and try to plant a kiss on my lips. I let her do it a few times, but the smell of tobacco made it difficult for me to breathe. Nammaw stopped giving kisses after I told her the smell made me sick to my stomach. She seemed disappointed as I turned my head and offered a cheek for her to kiss instead.

Now, as I lay next to Nammaw Jean and stroked her hair, I wondered if she knew I was there. Could she feel my hand stroking the hair away from her forehead?

As my fingers touched her silky hair, I analyzed the texture of Nammaw's skin. It had few wrinkles for a seventy-two-year-old woman who had been through years of inner turmoil. I wondered if she was dreaming, perhaps about people in her life she had lost — her parents, her son Gary — or those of us who were still with her. Was she still hanging onto life for a reason?

When I was young, she had regaled my family with stories of how she climbed a water tower as a little girl. She described how tall the tower had been, how narrow its metal ladder was. I suspected it all was a myth, not because I couldn't see her doing it, but because Nammaw didn't make eye contact as she told it. Her far-away gaze made me distrust her stories...and made me sad she had to keep telling them.

More than anything, I didn't want to turn out like Nammaw Jean. Most of my life, I disowned her for the mental illness she carried that could be passed on for generations. Whoever hadn't inherited her illness was haunted by those who had.

I began to cry. Not scant tears shed out of respectful sympathy for a dying loved one. These were thick, regretful tears. Regret at not having called Nammaw Jean on her birthday last year. Regret at laughing at her behind her back ever since I was ten years old. Regret at once having wished she wasn't my grandmother. Regret for despising her for so long because of her manic depression.

It all welled from a pool deep inside me and flowed out in violent tears that streaked my face and ran down my neck.

Then my words came out. Like the tears, I couldn't control

them. They spilled into the room, filling the quietness with a message that seemed to have been dictated by God himself.

"Nammaw, it wasn't your fault."

It was the message that had been wrenching my stomach for years and I didn't even know it. "You did the best you could, Nammaw."

The ease of being able to say those words and actually mean them filled me with peace. It wasn't her fault; Nammaw hadn't chosen depression for herself. Lying beside her, I finally accepted it.

"I love you. I've always loved you," I said.

Trembling, I put my lips on Nammaw's chapped lips. Her mouth gaped open as I lightly kissed her, her breath flowing softly in and out. I lay my head beside Nammaw Jean. Her eyebrows moved into two high arches above her closed eyes. They remained like that for a few seconds and then lowered.

Nammaw Jean heard me.

～

"You ready for a break?"

I rolled over as Roger walked in carrying a steaming cup of coffee with a magazine tucked under his arm.

"Couldn't sleep," he said, taking a sip.

I had trouble too. In the middle of the night, Nammaw's left arm shot up toward the ceiling, as if she was hanging on to an imaginary rope. Her fist clenched; her arm tightened. She kept her eyes closed and her mouth wide, holding her arm in a fixed position for several seconds. I tried to lower her arm and bring it back to her side, but she wouldn't budge, as if reaching for something that would pull her out of the bed to a place where she wouldn't feel any more pain.

Roger interrupted my thoughts. "If you're ready, I've got the key to Nammaw's apartment and I'll walk you over there."

The oxygen machine hummed as I grabbed my coat from the room's only chair and wrapped my body in the coat's wool warmth. I picked up my small suitcase, walked over to Nammaw and kissed the smooth skin on her forehead.

"Goodbye," I whispered in her ear.

Roger and I stepped out of the nursing home door and into the cool night air. We walked the hundred or so feet to Nammaw's apartment complex. A yellow porch light guided him as he turned the key in the lock.

"You're welcome to use her phone if you wanna call anyone later," he said. He opened the door, stepped inside and then pulled out a cigarette from his pocket, lighting it. The smoke blowing out the open door.

"Ya know, it's really great you made it down here. I'm glad you came." He looked at his shoes as he spoke. "It hasn't always been easy for your grandmother. It hasn't been easy, period. I just hope now she can find some peace."

He placed the cigarette between his lips and inhaled, releasing a cloud of smoke into the air. "I guess you heard there won't be a funeral service. She wants her body donated to science. Interesting, huh?"

He took a final drag then flicked the cigarette onto the paved drive in front of Nammaw's home. I watched the tip touch the ground, the wind snuffing it out.

"I'd better be getting back," he said. "I don't feel right leaving her there alone. You'll be okay, won't you?"

I assured him I would and closed the door. The apartment was a small studio. An entertainment center with rows of framed pictures faced the recliner. The couch sat against the picture window where Nammaw displayed her porcelain animal knickknacks. A vanity table and box of papers wedged in the corner. The small kitchen and bathroom were the only partitioned rooms.

I didn't feel tired, but I changed out of my clothes and put on pajamas anyway and then paced the apartment looking at Nammaw's treasures.

One of those items was a small framed snapshot sitting on her vanity. A man with shoulder-length hair and a brown mustache covering his upper lip watched a boy playing on the floor. It was one of the last photos of Uncle Gary taken the Thanksgiving before he died. The boy looked like Roger.

How had Gary really died? Nammaw once said someone gave him some drugs that killed him. But when Dad and I talked about it, he said how no one knew the extent of Gary's problems before he died. "No mother wants to believe her child could have overdosed," Dad said. "It's just too painful to accept."

A lower shelf held a black and white photo I had never seen. A man and woman held a small girl. The man and young girl flashed pleasant smiles, but the woman had a solemn expression, her lips pursed. It was my great-grandparents. The little girl was Nammaw Jean.

Beside the old picture was a color photograph. A young woman sat on a window ledge in a full white dress and held a bouquet of silk white roses. The photo was taken the day Ron and I walked down the aisle.

I didn't realize Nammaw Jean had my wedding photo or that she placed it beside the photo of her parents. Since she didn't attend our wedding, I figured Nammaw didn't have any photos.

The dark green and pink comforter on her bed smelled

like her favorite perfume from the drugstore, Liz Taylor's White Diamonds, and several years' worth of cigarette smoke. I reached over to turn out the lamp, eased under the blanket, and lay my head on Nammaw's pillow.

The apartment was completely dark and as silent as a dying woman's fragile breath. This was Nammaw Jean's home.

For one night, it would be my own.

11 Ten Teeny, Tiny Signing Fingers

Confession: You can teach a lip-reading mom new tricks.

Mom asked me to give the eulogy and to sing a song at Nammaw Jean's memorial service.

Before my hearing-loss diagnosis, I sang in church choirs. I played clarinet in junior high band and serenaded my parents twice a week on my squeaky horn. I performed dramatic and comedic duets in high school and gave a speech in front of my graduating senior class.

None of this mattered when I stepped onto the stage to deliver Nammaw's eulogy. I was terrified of holding a microphone and speaking into it with my ears not able to hear well.

It was a family service, so Ron and I brought baby Reagan and Nicklaus along for the bumpy ride. When the minister spoke about my grandma once bribing him with money to buy her a pack of cigarettes, I just about slid out of my seat.

"Ah yes, he chuckled. "That Jean knew what she wanted and, my word did she have stories to share."

What kinds of stories? My eyes grew the size of saucers envisioning her talking up a few tall tales.

Pastor Bribes shook his head, grinning. "Every time the television set showed a starving kid, Jean was divvying up cash to send 'em. 'Whoa, whoa,' I told her. 'You got money to live on?' She says, 'Ah boy, do I. Got a good retirement from that work I did for the electric company.' I say, 'So you got that kinda money and you live in this small apartment?"

"Enough of my storytelling," he laughed, waving his hands. "Let's hear from someone who knew her best."

As I got up and walked toward him, he glanced at a clock in the back of the sanctuary. I had just made a New Year's resolution to stop feeling sorry for myself. After Nammaw Jean died and I started taking happy pills, my focus shifted to seeing bright colors in the darkness and sunshine on gray February days. I realized being a depressed hard-of-hearing mom in recovery wasn't the end of life.

I took to the stage like Joan of Arc, determined to feign courage and address the crowd with words of comfort, wisdom, and sincerity.

Truth: I hadn't written anything down, nor did I have the faintest idea of how to comfort everyone. "Um, hello. My grandma died from eating too many sweets and not taking care of herself." Nope. I would have to invent a story.

I scanned the audience members — all twelve of them — and made eye contact with a fake potted plant at the back of the auditorium.

"My name is Shanna. I'm Jean's granddaughter." I drew in a deep breath and let it out. "What I want to say is, well — I guess I should say that, um..."

Mom coughed. Nicklaus fidgeted with a plastic water bottle in his seat. Reagan cooed in Ron's lap. Pastor Bribes stared at the wall clock. Tick tock.

"I should say that my grandmother took me to church, when I visited her."

Was I speaking loud enough into the microphone? Too

loud? Was the thing even turned on?

My flawed ears heard more of the background noise than what I struggled to say. Mom let out another raspy cough. Someone's feet clanked against the back of a pew. I looked over, and Nicklaus had taken a swig from the water bottle.

"She took me and my sisters to Sunday school and Bible school. When we were little girls. She used to, um..."

Reagan let out a full-blown, floor-vibrating scream. I watched Ron whisk her to the back of the room where he stood by a fake plant trying to hush our girl.

"My grandmother used to put our hair in rollers, the night before going to church. She'd lean our heads over the sink and get our hair wet. Then she'd wrap our wet hair in the rollers. We'd sleep in these pink foam things all night. In the morning, she'd take out the rollers, and our hair would be these full of damp ringlets."

Mom let out yet another cough. Then another. Then a much longer one — a gagging noise as her entire body shook.

The pastor skipped up to my microphone. "Anybody got any water?"

Nicklaus was still toying with the plastic water bottle, so I motioned for someone to grab it, but when Mom tried to swallow from the bottle, nothing came out. She continued gag-coughing.

"Anybody got a cough drop?" he asked.

Someone brought Mom one, and when the gagging subsided, she got up, walked slowly to the back of the auditorium, to stand next to Ron and Reagan.

"Ready to sing?" the pastor whispered as he picked up a portable CD player and planted it on the podium in front of me. I reached underneath and grabbed my recorded copy of

"Amazing Grace" instrumentals.

"How 'bout we join along with you?" he said.

Before I could answer, he directed everyone to page one-hundred-and-something in the church hymnal. I slid the CD in the player, pressed play, and hoped the volume was turned up loud enough to mask my warbling voice.

As I sang, "How sweet the sound..." I scanned the audience for their reactions to my likely off-key singing. Most sat with their noses buried in their hymnals. Lydia didn't sing, but I could count on one hand the number of times I'd seen her join in a song.

If Janie had been there, we would have exchanged amused glances, then dissolved into nervous giggles right there on the stage. Janie wasn't there. None of us had heard from her in a week, nor knew where she was.

⁓

Some days, it was simply easier to live in the past. On those days, I called up my friend, Hannah. Friends since the sixth grade, we bonded over our similar names, love of boys, and passion for Wilson Phillips songs.

Hannah was the reason I cut my hair pixie short like singer Chynna Phillips, circa 1990. Prior to the cut, I sat in on one of Hannah's high school cosmetology classes. She persuaded me to be her guinea pig for a curly-do perm. I later learned it was the first hair permanent she had ever given.

When I came out of Hannah's lab, my board-straight hair was wavy-soft in the back — and burned to a crisp where my bangs used to hang. A couple of hair-washings later, my waves dissolved to half-fluff, half-frizz. After a trip to the beauty shop, a professional stylist snipped my burnt ends into a feathery 'do worthy of the Wilson Phillips Hair Hall of Shame.

Even if the cosmetology arrangement didn't work out for me and Hannah, our friendship did. I dialed her up via my amplified phone.

"Hannah, we need a heart to heart. It's about Janie."

Whenever I called her up about Janie, Hannah did most of the listening while I talked.

"Go on," she said.

"You know, we still don't know where Janie is. She has no phone, no address. She didn't so much as send a sympathy card when Nammaw died."

"Yeah," Hannah said.

"Well, I got this post card from her. It was of a waterfall, and on the back side the postmark was from Vegas. Now, how in the world did Janie end up in Vegas?"

"Uh-huh."

"So I asked Mom. Turns out Janie met some guy, and he had business in Vegas. He also had some business in Massachusetts, Oklahoma. 'What kind of business is it?' I asked Mom...she wouldn't tell me, but I knew... Hannah, I think this guy's a dealer."

"Drugs?"

"That's the reason Janie didn't make Nammaw's service. That's the reason we don't have a number or address. Janie is on the road with this dealer."

"Are you sure?"

"You tell me this: How did Janie pay for that tattoo on her neck, the one Mom said she had last time she saw her? Janie hasn't worked a steady job in months. How does she get her clothes? How does she pay for food? Gas in the car?"

"Yeah."

"The sad part, Hannah. This is the part that breaks my heart. What's gonna happen to Janie's girls?"

My sister married three times and gave birth to three girls. Callie and Cara, her twins, were now living with their father thousands of miles away. Little Annie lived with a different dad in another state. Mom and Dad helped raise Janie's girls.

The last memory I had of them with their mother, Janie sat on a worn couch in their trailer. While the girls munched on handfuls of Cap'n Crunch cereal straight out of the box, Janie glared at the television. She wore a tattered sweatshirt and shook nervously. When I spoke to Janie, she didn't answer or look at me. When I left, Callie and Cara gazed at me through the torn screen window. They seemed helpless and hungry, and I wanted to whisk them away from their filthy trailer.

State authorities were called a couple of weeks later, and Callie, Cara, and Annie went to live with their fathers. Janie stuck around long enough to gut out her trailer. She stole Mom's wedding ring and threatened to ram her car into my parents' house before disappearing.

"You know the sad part?" I propped Reagan onto my shoulder. "I don't know how to pray for her."

"What do you mean?"

I patted the baby's back. "Sometimes I pray she'll be well, come back, and be a good momma to her girls. Other times, I pray God would just take her. Just take her home."

"Home?"

"The only way she will have no more pain is if God takes her."

I remembered driving with Nicklaus and Reagan snug in their car seats. It was not long after I got help for my depression. Nicklaus snuggled into his seat with his bulky coat and dozed off. I couldn't see Reagan's face through the rearview mirror because her car seat faced the back, but I assumed she was sleeping since she was quiet. For the first time since bringing Reagan home from the hospital, I realized I now had two kids to love. Two. My love had multiplied, and I loved each of my children in special and different ways. But I loved them with the same protective love. I would die for them.

"Janie couldn't take care of her girls," I said to Hannah. "I don't understand. I just don't understand."

~

I took refuge in my journal. It became the place where I tucked away my memories, dreams, and odd observations.

February 28

I had an encounter today with a stranger. The first thing I noticed about her was her eyes — blue like the open sky. She held a boy, not older than two, presumably her son. A solid brown birthmark colored the right lower half of his face.

She looked at me, still holding her son, her eyes protective yet vulnerable. Protective of the son she must shield from onlookers' curious stares. Vulnerable about her role as a mother and why anyone would be looking at her.

It wasn't her son that caught my attention, it was her eyes. This woman looked just like Janie — only she resembled my sister in much healthier days. The woman's golden blonde hair, parted straight down the

125

middle, matched my sister's carefree hairstyle back in high school. The woman's eyes were set wide apart, and her nose appeared slightly congested. Her lower lip was slightly fuller than the upper lip. Straight rows of white teeth were revealed from behind her pouty expression.

If only it had been Janie.

The years haven't been kind to my sister. Golden hair has been bleached a white blonde, short spikes of hair mismatched her blushing pink face. The pouty lips are now chapped, with top teeth constantly biting at her lower lip. Janie's nose has become narrower, bonier — separating her milky blue eyes at its topmost peak. Their sky color is clouded in gray undertones, the color of lost hope.

I wanted to embrace this stranger. She obviously loved her child. She seemed like the idea of what Janie could have been if she had chosen to see the world through love, instead of confusion.

March 9

My earliest childhood memory was sitting in the back seat of Mom and Dad's Malibu, waiting to leave the hospital. Our new baby was less than a week old, swaddled in a blanket. Mom held her in the front seat.

Lydia was barely old enough to see above the seat when she stretched on her tippy toes. She stared at this baby. Tufts of red hair sprouted from the newborn's head. Her face was slim, her cheeks rosy. Her long lashes rested, so I couldn't see her eyes.

Mom raised the baby up for Lydia and me to see. "Just look at your baby sister," she said.

Baby lay like a cocoon inside her soft pink blanket. I imagined her kicking her toes and legs to free herself, just like a butterfly. It was seventy degrees, sunny and too warm for a blanket cocoon.

I wasn't allowed in the hospital when Baby was born. Hospital's orders. Little kids weren't allowed past the doors unless they were sick or dying.

Lydia leaned over the seat to get a better view. She didn't look anything like Baby, with her dull brown wavy hair and fringe of bangs that curled under by themselves. I had paper-straight wheat-colored hair that didn't match Baby's either. The only way I'd have curls is if I slept in foam rollers, which I did practically every night.

"Would you just look at her," Mom said.

Lydia leaned into Mom's seat, her eyes sparkling with love. "Hi, Baby Sister."

I was two-and-a-half years younger and four inches shorter than Lydia. No matter how much I stretched, I had a hard time seeing Baby over the seat.

"That's your Big Sister," Mom said to Baby. She pointed to Lydia. "She's going to be your second mom."

Lydia smiled in a way that made my cheeks turn red. My face was on fire.

"Can I hold her?" Lydia asked.

"Sure," Mom said.

I reached over the seat as far as I could. My nose pressed into the headrest cushion. "Can I hold her?"

Mom lifted Baby over the seat where Lydia waited with outstretched arms.

"Not now," Mom said.

From the beginning, I was jealous of Baby.

Growing up, I never let her forget. I pinched her, pushed her, dug my fingernails into her skin and dared her to walk across loose boards in the backyard.

Still, nothing changed. Long into our adult years, with kids of our own, the role of Baby was always Janie's.

"How do you love us, flaws and all?" I asked God during one of my pray-while-driving sessions. It had become a habit to pray, in my head, while taking Nicklaus to play dates or shuffling Reagan to doctors' checkup visits. I needed an outlet for my frustration, besides the phone and my journal. I needed to keep busy.

Questions gushed through my head like water. "How do you feel when we mess up, God?" "What happens if a person loses her way but once loved you deeply?" I thought of Janie.

"Why can't I hear my child coo in the back seat?"

Through the rearview mirror, I watched her lips move while she played in her new car seat. She held a pink cloth dolly in one hand, intermittently sucking her thumb.

When I read the ad for a baby sign-language class, I signed right up. I couldn't hear Reagan well. I needed a communication backup in case I became stone deaf.

"God, why is this happening to me?"

I pulled the car into a small lot facing a bowling alley and shopping center. The sign out front read, "Hollyville Learning Center." I gazed at Reagan in the rearview mirror. "You ready to learn how to talk to Mommy, Baby Girl?"

Reagan plopped her thumb into her mouth. Dressed in a flowing Laura Ingalls' style skirt and jean jacket, a fancy scarlet bow clipped into her barely-there hair, Reagan was dressed to the nines for her first baby sign class. But her smelly diaper told a different story. Running late, as usual, I had forgotten to change it.

"I'm such a mess," I whispered to God. To myself.

After a quick stroll down the deserted halls of the learning center, I found the restrooms. This place reminded me not so much as a school, but as an institution. "What am I doing, God?"

As I pulled down Reagan's skirt to reveal her dirty diaper, I couldn't help but wonder... What kind of mom would I be without the ability to hear?

Reagan's thumb dangled out of the corner of her mouth.

"Can you tell me, Baby Girl?" I rubbed her bottom with a wet wipe. It had also become a habit to ask her questions as I changed her diapers. Reagan's sky blue eyes met my nervous gaze. Her lips let go of the thumb, the wet finger glistened with saliva.

She cooed something to me I couldn't understand.

"Oh, really?" I said, pulling up her skirt. "Is that what you think, Baby Girl?"

There we were...two human beings who desperately wanted to understand one another, to communicate clearly. The answer rested in baby sign language. I was sure of it. The nice gal at the library told me all about it. She even showed me shelves of sign language videos developed just for babies and toddlers. Within a month, I had checked out all those videos from the library.

I patted Reagan's back as we roamed the hallways. Neon-colored signs with arrows showed us which direction to go. At the end of one empty hallway was an open door with a glowing classroom light. The sign read, "Baby Signing Time."

Before I stepped through the open door, my hearing aids picked up the sound of playful mom and baby bantering inside. "Oh, oh, oh! Coo, coo, coo!"

A woman wearing spectacles with a cute dark cropped hairdo waved us in. "I'm Miss Melanie," she said in a bubbly voice. "And you are?"

The room was packed, wall-to-wall, with moms, grandmas, nannies, aunts, one dad, and a dozen babies and young toddlers. Most of the grownups sat on the floor, Indian style, with babies at their hips. A couple of stressed-out mommies raced around the room, chasing after their newly walking toddlers.

"This is Reagan. I'm her mom."

"Hello, Reagan and Reagan's mom." Miss Melanie picked up sticky name tags and a marker. "Take these...and these."

Miss Melanie grabbed a stapled stack of paper and handed it to me. The first sheet read "Sign Language Alphabet." It was filled with illustrations of different hand motions.

"Do you know any sign?" Miss Melanie asked.

In college, two girls in the dorm were deaf education majors. While walking to class or eating in the cafeteria, they practiced signing to each other. "How are you?" they'd sign to me. "What is your name?" I pretended to know what they had signed, nod, and smile. Only later did they start using their voices when they signed to me. That's when I started picking up on their special language. I learned a handful of signs, most of them relating to "how are you" and "what is your name." I even learned how to spell my name in sign language, using the finger signs. But I hadn't practiced signing in ten years.

"Not much."

Reagan and I found an empty spot on the carpet next to a stressed-out mommy wrestling her son into a sitting position. On the other side of us was a young woman with her hair pulled into a ponytail. When I glanced at her, not a speck of makeup was on her face. She didn't need it. Her coffee-colored skin was flawless.

"I'm Shanna," I said, reaching out my hand to her.

"Isabella." She shook my hand. "This is Dominique."

I waved at the little boy, and he waved back.

"He's 14 months," Isabella said. "How old is your girl?"

Reagan sat at my hip, her thumb back in her mouth. "Eight months."

"Wow, she's a young one."

"Yeah."

What did Isabella really mean — that Reagan was too young for the class?

"Good morning, everyone. I'm Miss Melanie. And I want to welcome you to the first session of Baby Signing Time."

The ladies around me politely clapped. Miss Melanie waved her hands as she spoke. Was she signing to us?

"Do we have anyone here who's taken my classes before?" she spoke and signed.

A few hands shot up from around the room, including Isabella's. Uh-huh. That's why Isabella seemed so calm. She was a regular of Miss Melanie's.

"In today's class, we're going to focus on introducing ourselves. We're going to learn the signs for our names." Miss Melanie held up her copy of the handout that read, "Sign Language Alphabet" then set it down.

She placed her hand to her chest. "My name." She stacked

her middle and pointer fingers in front of her. "Is Miss Mela-nie." She curled one hand into a fist with the thumb poking out between the ring finger and pinky. "That's the sign for the letter 'M.'"

In college, the girls in the dorm gave me the nickname "Curly Shanna" because I wore an awful perm my freshman and sophomore years. Even when I let the curls grow out and my hair was back to being stick-straight, the nickname stuck. In sign language, my name was Curly S, which was the sign letter 'S' (a fist with the thumb in front of the fingers) making curly motions next to my head.

No one in Baby Signing Time would see me sign this hor-rific nickname.

"My name," Isabella said to Dominique. "Do you remem-ber?" Dominique, with his thick and wavy Hershey bar-colored hair, showed his mom the sign for 'D.'

"Good boy," Isabella said, kissing his forehead. Ugh.

I turned Reagan to face me.

"Baby Girl," I said, glaring at the Sign Language Alphabet handout. "Your name is..."

I crossed my pointer and middle fingers — the sign for "R."

"Can you do it?" I asked.

I pried her thumb out of her mouth, took that hand, and gently moved her fingers to cross them.

"Reagan," I said. "'R' is for Rea-gan." My words were as slow and over-enunciated as that annoying guy Denny who fitted me with my hearing aids. Can. You. Hear. Me?

Isabella waved at me. "That's not the sign for 'R.' Move her fingers this way."

She yanked Reagan's other hand and curled her pointer and middle fingers into perfect form.

"Are you sure she's ready for this class?" Isabella said.

I forced a grin.

What was the sign for 'Shut up'?

~

March 16

Why is motherhood such a roller coaster experience?

There is the tired exhilaration of birth, followed by postpartum pain and moments of joy. There is unexplained crying over little things and heart flutters over big things. The excitement over milestones and precious memories. The grief over milestones since time passes too quickly.

In the moment a new life is born, there is also newness for the mother and the incomprehensible death of her life as she knew it before. Why can't the journey be a consistent state of calmness instead of the ups and downs of unpredictable emotion?

Why is motherhood the most joyful and gutwrenching experience I've ever known?

~

I called up Hannah to vent about baby sign class, along with all my roller coaster emotions.

"Look up Isaiah 63," she said. "It will help you drive out all this junk you feel."

"What?"

"Trust me," Hannah said.

While Nicklaus and Reagan napped, I pulled out my tattered Bible Mom gave me when I was fourteen. In junior high, I read it every day. In high school, I opened it most days. After that? Not so much.

It took a while to find Isaiah.

"Chapter 63, verse nine," I read. "In all their distress he too was distressed."

Who was "he?" Oh yeah. God.

"In all their distress he too was distressed, and the angel of his presence saved them."

Angel of his what? How could God have an angel going around saving everybody? I thought angels were fairytale creatures, like in books and cheesy TV shows.

How could this angel save them? What would it do — float down from the sky, wrap its feathers around people, and whisk them off to Fairytale Land?

What in the world did it all mean?

12 Speak Clearly into the Microphone

Confession: Gimme a taste of that mic.

Worrywart should have been my middle name. My childhood was defined by weight worries, fitting-in-at-school concerns, academic anguish, and so on. I was nine years old when I subscribed to *Weight Watchers* magazine and exercised to Richard Simmons: Sweating to the Oldies. I worried my belly pooched out too much in my Smurfette nightgown.

Forget peer pressure. I put enough on myself to make the most A's in third grade. While the girls at school had sleepovers, ate pizza, and phoned boys they crushed on, I stayed home. I'd lay stomach-down on my bed, stressing over spelling homework on Friday nights.

Now, I worried about being a good mom.

The round table was elbow-to-elbow with other mommies likely stressing about the same thing. They called our group MOPS, an acronym for Mothers of Preschoolers. Twice a month on Tuesday mornings, I strained to hear this group of women share about the highs and lows of suburban mommyhood.

To blend in, I kept my hair long, covering my ears and the hearing aids that revealed something was wrong with me. I dressed in my most expensive sweaters and shoes, and wore a full face of makeup. Getting ready for MOPS was like getting ready for a job interview.

"Shanna," Hailey announced one Tuesday morning. "We are looking for moms to share their stories. Since you are new, would you like to share yours?"

Hailey, with her natural platinum blonde head of curls, was the epitome of a MOP. Each morning from a stage, she welcomed other moms at our church into this social circle of mothering. Hailey pressed all her cotton T-shirts before stepping foot on the stage, and her jeans hugged her fit body. As the mother of two smiling, giggling boys, she exemplified parenting perfection.

I looked around the table at the other moms, all gazing at me with curious expressions. Maybe they were hoping I would reveal more of myself beyond the polished plum lipstick I wore that morning.

"I guess," I said to Hailey. What was I doing?

Two months later, I sat in the ladies restroom at church.

"What am I doing?" My thoughts spewed out in a nervous, breathy whisper. I stared at my reflection in the mirror. In order to share my story with the MOPS that morning, I opted to dress the part of a princess. Literally.

I wore the cream and sparkly iridescent bridesmaid's gown that my lifelong friend, Hannah, purchased for me to wear in her wedding years before. With my heels, the dress was an inch too long and the skirt sported a black tar mark where I stepped on it one too many times in the asphalted parking lot.

The dress was the least of my worries. How should I wear my hair?

At Hannah's wedding, my strands were teased into an up-do just like all the other bridesmaids. After several spritzes of hairspray and bobby pins, my hair remained flawless even after the ceremony and well past all the dancing at Hannah's reception. My hair was so thick, it required more bobby pins and spray than any of the other bridesmaids.

How in the world was I going to fix my hair with these hearing aids behind my ears? A formal dress required an upscale updo, but as soon as the strands were teased into the updo, they revealed a part of myself I wanted to hide.

The hearing aids weren't pretty. They weren't even interesting. They were bland and boring and obnoxious and downright ugly. How could I dress up hearing aids that matched the color of hardened oatmeal and stuck out a quarter-inch from behind each ear? I had Dumbo ears when I wore my hearing aids since the blasted devices pushed my earlobes away from my head. The hard ear molds that rested uncomfortably inside my ears weren't attractive either. Their clear color began to turn a beeswax yellow with all the earwax buildup that couldn't be removed.

I toyed with my hair just as much as I toyed with my thoughts. Would the moms laugh at my hearing aids? Would they look at me differently once I revealed them? Would I appear weird to them once I came out of the hearing-loss closet? Would anyone even notice?

I hoped for the latter as I wrestled my hair into an updo worthy of a catwalk model.

"And now," Hailey announced from the microphone. "One of our newest moms will share her story about what brought her to MOPS. Some of you may already know her. But for those of you who don't, we are going to learn more about Ms. Shanna Groves."

The church fellowship hall rumbled with applause. My

stomach rumbled with acid indigestion. I closed my eyes and mumbled, "Here goes nothing."

From the back of the room, I waltzed toward the stage in my formal attire. "I am a princess, I am a princess," I sang.

Because my eyes were partially closed, I didn't see what I assumed were shocked stares coming my way, nor could I count the number of times I tripped on my hemline.

Out of the corner of my eye, I glimpsed the stage as I pranced up the steps and nearly did a nose-dive after stepping on my skirt.

"Good morning," I said into the microphone. The audience was completely silent.

Wasn't this the part where the moms should laugh at my crazy, dancing, dressed-up antics? I wore a tiara and held a plastic scepter. Wouldn't they chuckle at this outlandish attire? Maybe they were confused. Or, maybe they didn't see the hearing aids since I stood several feet away on a stage.

My stomach tickled with nerves. This was my moment to share a story.

"The reason I'm standing here today, in this silly costume, is because I have a secret to share."

On an impulse, I fidgeted with one of my hearing aids, pulled it out from behind my ear and cupped it in my hand.

"Most of you have never seen me dressed like this with my hair in an updo."

My thumb rubbed the hearing aid in my hand.

"That's because I didn't want you to see my ears."

With the hearing aid in hand, I raised it high above my head and let the stage lighting shine on my oatmeal-colored listening device.

"I wear hearing aids. I have for a couple of years."

The moms glared at my hearing aid, as if I held a detonated bomb. Or maybe I imagined that they did. My thoughts played tricks with me.

"Several years ago, right after my son was born, I learned that I was going deaf. No explanation as to why."

Dressed in my ridiculous bridesmaid's dress, I managed not to trip off the stage after finishing the story. The applause, even with one of my hearing aids taken out and still cupped inside my hand, was deafening.

During the weeks after my speech, I met others with special needs. They came to me one at a time. Sometimes, they came in pairs. Sometimes in droves.

Patricia walked into one of our MOPS meetings with an obvious limp. As she poured a cup of coffee, I noticed her left hand lay unused.

"I had a stroke two years ago, when my youngest daughter was 13 months old," she wrote me after my MOPS speech. "I had just quit work to become a stay-at-home mom. The stroke paralyzed the left side of my body.

"Before you spoke," Patricia added, "I thought I was the only young mom in the world with a disability."

Disability? Did that word describe my hearing loss? Was I disabled from enjoying all the sounds around me? Was Patricia disabled from picking up her daughter with both arms, or pouring herself a cup of coffee with her left hand?

"You made me feel like I wasn't alone." Her e-mail was typed in all caps because, as she pointed out, she could only type with one hand.

Patricia and I bonded over our special needs. When we engaged in conversations with other moms, she became a second set of ears for me — repeating things I hadn't understood. When we lifted our kids out of their car seats, I helped Patricia with my hands — buckling or unbuckling her daughter's seat belt.

Becky confided she had fought depression her entire life. "When you shared with the group like that," she said to me when we were alone, "I knew you got it."

We swapped depression treatment stories.

"The manufacturer of my medicine stopped making it," she said as we delivered boxes of clothes to a MOPS family in need. "I never have found another medicine that helps me."

With our kids crammed into the backseat of my SUV, Becky and I drove to a part of town most people would never set foot in after dark.

"LOCAL FAMILY HOMELESS," read the story in our church bulletin. "FATHER OF SEVEN GIRLS NEEDS HOME, CAR, FOOD, AND CLOTHES."

Someone from the church provided a two-bedroom apartment rent free. Another family donated a mint-condition Suburban for the father to drive. Someone else offered him a job. A local food pantry stocked their donated refrigerator.

Seven boxes and trash bags — one stuffed for each girl — sat in the trunk of my car. When Becky and I pulled into the row of modest apartments on Loula Street, one of the battered front doors opened for us.

A short man with a pencil-thin mustache walked toward us.

"I Miguel. Miguel Martinez," he said, extending his hand. "Thank you for clothes. Girls so happy."

International accents were a challenge to understand. I caught maybe a tenth of what came out of the person's mouth.

I struggled to understand Miguel's halted use of the English language. When he spoke, I remained silent, nodding and smiling along with his accented words.

Becky stayed by the SUV with the kids while Miguel and I took the boxes and bags inside.

The first child to greet me inside the house was the oldest daughter, who appeared to be eleven or twelve years old. She greeted me with a nod as she brushed one of her sister's thick manes of chocolate brown hair. Another girl, who I presumed was the second oldest, entertained the other girls by switching channels on a beat-up TV. One of the younger girls, about age three, held the crying baby.

Miguel carried his boxes into a back bedroom. Inside were two sets of bunk beds, each pushed against a wall. A crib wedged in between.

"Church give us beds," he said, motioning to the bunk beds, which held two pillows each. The girls must have shared each bed. "When me wife gone, we got nothing."

I sat my box down on one of the beds. "I'm sorry she left."

Miguel squinted at me.

"I mean, I'm sorry." I bit my lip.

Miguel shoved his box into the room's only bed-less corner.

"She...what is word? She disappear. She sad. After having baby. She disappear."

After saying goodbye to Miguel and his girls, I knew it wasn't a permanent goodbye. I would see this family again. I had to see them again.

As Becky and I drove away, Miguel's words tossed around in my mind. "She sad. After having baby. She disappear."

I thought about the months I couldn't nurture baby Reagan because I was so sad. About my sister Janie's bouts with depression and drugs; her depression accelerated after the birth of her youngest daughter. About Patricia and the anguish she felt at not being able to hold her child because of her stroke. About Becky's lingering sadness at not being able to find the right depression treatment.

I thought about the two years my stomach remained in knots while I waited to come out of the closet with hearing loss. The stress of trying to lip-read my two children — an impossible task at times. The phone calls with Mom, garbled because of my inability to understand her words.

With each thought that rolled through my brain, something powerful built inside me. It was a heightened awareness of other people's needs. It was also the sense I could help these people. I couldn't bring back the mom who disappeared from the Martinez family, but I could encourage her seven daughters by giving them clothes.

I couldn't release Janie from the crippling hold of drug dependency, or save her from the homeless shelter in which she'd spent the last month. But I could encourage her in seeking professional help.

Nor could I heal Patricia of her stroke or cure Becky of her depression. But I could be Patricia's hands to unbuckle her daughter's car seat. And I could drive my SUV around the shady part of town and let Becky vent her frustrations. Hearing loss or not, depression or not, I was still able to help my friends.

I just had to have courage.

⁓

The house next door to us sold in a month.

As the new home owners unloaded furniture and boxes, I

spied on them from my garage. Two women appeared from a car, carrying bags of odds and ends. One of them appeared about my age, her raven black hair pulled into a ponytail. Something interesting rested behind one of her ears.

Was I hallucinating? Was this person wearing a hearing aid?

I stepped out of the garage. "Hi. I'm Shanna."

The woman with the hearing aid continued walking, oblivious to my presence.

"Hello!" I shouted. "Welcome to the neighborhood."

The other woman, who appeared to be in her fifties, walked over.

"Hi Shanna." She extended her hand. "I'm just helping my daughter and son-in-law move in."

"Is that your daughter, the one wearing..."

The woman smiled. "Yes, that's my daughter. I'll introduce you." We walked in the house. The woman stepped behind the young woman with the raven-black ponytail and tapped her shoulder.

"Sweetheart," the older woman said to her daughter. "I. Want. You. To. Meet. Shan-na."

What was this? The woman spoke in the same tone I once dreaded when people first learned of my hearing loss.

Two glistening objects rested behind the young woman's ears. Two hearing aids, twice the size of my own.

"You wear them," I said to her.

The young woman stared at me, confused.

I pointed to my ears. "I wear hearing aids too."

I lifted my hair to give her a better view of my oatmeal-colored listening devices.

She grinned. "I'm Miranda, but friends call me Mandy."

It was an incredible offer.

My MOPS friend, Becky, offered to watch Miguel Martinez's three toddlers, whom she barely knew. Miguel worked ten-hour shifts at his new job. While his older girls attended school, church volunteers cared for the younger ones. Every day's childcare was arranged for that particular week, except Monday.

"I'll have to bring my boy along with me," Becky explained over the phone. "But I'll be there at 7:30 and stay until 5:30."

Becky and I met at Miguel's apartment to make sure she could handle this task. Her oversized purse was filled with all her personal belongings, along with a loaf of bread and jar of peanut butter. "In case the girls need food," she said.

My friend watched those girls once a week for the next month — free of charge.

At Christmas, our group of MOPS moms added the girls to our holiday shopping lists. We donated a five-foot artificial tree, strands of lights, garland, and ornaments. Seven of us even gathered in the Martinez home for a tree-trimming party.

"Go get some coffee," we told Miguel as we kicked him out of his apartment.

Each mom presented the girls with two wrapped presents — a gift of clothes, a gift of toys.

Someone brought a portable CD player and her Frank Sinatra Christmas album. Someone else prepared mugs of cocoa, while the rest of us took turns decorating holiday cookies with our adopted girl.

At times, obstacles and self-doubt prevented me from helping. What was I doing watching another man's kids when taking care of my own two could be overwhelming? What would

Ron think of me sitting in a strange man's house? Why didn't some other mom help these girls — since their own mother had abandoned them?

It was difficult to understand why I had to be part of this group that helped the Martinez family. I didn't know Miguel and his daughters well, and I certainly couldn't understand their Latino accents.

I was a hard-of-hearing mom helping a hard-to-lip-read family.

~

I once saw an interesting acronym for the word TEAM: T - Together; E - Everyone; A - Accomplishes; M - More.

The only team experiences I had growing up were in debate and drama. I argued and acted with the best of them. Yet when attempting to play team sports, I spent most of my time on a bench.

Teamwork meant little to me, because I preferred to do things my own way. I was an individual, not a team player.

After I met my neighbor, Mandy, I began questioning this individualist mentality. She excelled in soccer throughout school, despite being born deaf. She pledged a sorority in college, attended parties, and met the love of her life, Sam, who also loved team sports. All of this, despite her being deaf.

Mandy spoke clearly and lip-read proficiently. Yet the moment she turned her head away and I attempted to engage in conversation, my words fell on deaf ears.

I learned she did so well in school, professionally, and in her love life because she thrived on teamwork. Her earliest team consisted of her parents. Her mom, a speech pathologist, taught Mandy early on how to clearly develop spoken language. Her dad, an avid traveler and outdoorsman, taught Mandy how to navigate unknown territory.

In spite of a profound hearing loss, she thrived.

"Can you help me?" I asked her. "I need help with this whole hearing-loss thing."

My new neighbor and I became regular coffee-drinking pals. Occasionally, one of us rented a captioned movie, and we'd hang out at each other's houses.

"Hearing loss is all I've ever known." Mandy spoke with an accent, which I learned came from her having a difficult time hearing her own voice.

"In grade school, I had a sign language interpreter who sat in the front of the class with me." Mandy moved her hands while she spoke. I wasn't sure if it was sign language or she simply liked to move her hands.

"In middle and high school, I had note takers. And an FM system. It had two parts — one that plugged into my hearing aids and the other part had a microphone that the teacher wore. It helped me hear the teacher better."

"So, what did you use in college?" I asked. Mandy has a master's degree in engineering.

"The FM system, note takers, and CART."

"What's CART?"

Mandy tapped her chin. "I'm trying to remember what it stands for. I think, Computer Assisted Realtime Translation — something like that. I had a laptop and someone who sat beside me and translated the professor's words by typing them. It's a service that colleges are supposed to offer. But you have to ask for it."

"So CART is like captions on the TV?"

"Pretty much," Mandy said.

"And all I need to do is ask for these captions?"

"Yep."

"So all I have to do is ask for help — if I don't hear something?"

"That's right."

I nodded. "Okay."

A few days later, I returned to the MOPS group with a determination to ask for help.

"Hailey," I said to our MOPS leader. "I'm having trouble hearing everything at our meetings. Like when you talk on the stage. I miss so much."

"The acoustics are bad in here," Hailey said, pointing to the room's high ceilings. "I've been wanting to move us into a different room for a long time, but we need this larger space."

"What can I do to help?"

Hailey's perfectly rouged lips widened into a smile. "Would you pray about being our new leader?"

"Huh?"

Hailey's smile didn't fade. "This is my last semester with MOPS. I really want to free up more of my time to spend with my family. I've been praying about this a long time, and I think God has chosen you to be the next leader of MOPS."

My thoughts raced. What kind of leader would I be — one who couldn't hear very well? God didn't use deaf moms to lead large groups. Did he?

13 My Near Crash with Death

Confession: Billy Graham was my co-pilot.

Sunday's sermon at church intrigued me.

"In seeking truth," our pastor said, "spiritual maturity pushes against spiritual falsehood."

Prior to Sunday's sermon or Hailey asking me to be the first lip-reading MOPS leader, prior to my bout with depression or Nammaw Jean's illness and untimely death, prior to my learning I was slowly going deaf — I had a plan.

That plan was to sink my teeth into writing something that would rattle the status quo. I wanted to be Lois Lane on steroids; Mrs. Clark Kent and Mrs. Superwoman. My writing would cure all death and destruction, all loneliness, all the junk that came with life. I wanted to author a book to stir souls and save the world.

As I flipped through the tattered Bible Mom had given me, I realized what I wanted to write had already been written.

"Now we see but a poor reflection as in a mirror," I read from the worn book of 1 Corinthians in the New Testament. "Then we shall see face to face."

What didn't make sense was how a book that lay unopened under my bed for the first half of my marriage now evoked such emotion.

"Now I know in part," wrote the author of this book. Paul, I believe. "Then I shall know fully, even as I am fully known."

Prior to all the uncertainty of my hearing loss, I had the future mapped out. I would script a book. About what, I didn't know. Then I'd spend the next three months soliciting book agents, in hopes of finding one to fall in love with my carefully written words. While the agent shopped my book to publishers, I'd draft my next book. It would be a sequel or companion piece to the first manuscript. Within a year, I'd be a published author with the second book in the can.

That didn't happen.

While Nammaw Jean convalesced in her hospice bed, I dreamed up a book idea. When I flew home after she died, I sat in front of the computer every day, typing thoughts and dreams for hours. The manuscript, "All Roads Lead to Home," was the story about finding my way back to Nammaw Jean and accepting our family's legacy of depression. It required hours of phone calls with Mom, Uncle Roger, and a few other relatives — Janie included.

She was strung out during some of our phone calls, but her message was crystal clear — "You've gotta write about our family depression."

So I did. While Reagan napped or bounced her exersaucer, I wrote. After Nicklaus and Reagan went to bed, I plopped myself in front of the computer.

Chapter One: A story about Nammaw Jean's mom, Gracie. My great-granddaddy, whose manic depression surfaced in the early 1930's. How he struggled to hold a job, forcing his wife — my great-grandma Gracie — to work long shifts as a nurse.

Chapter Two: The story of Nammaw Jean and her wedding day. The day she married my Papa Larry. He wasn't Mom's birth dad, but he eventually adopted her and became the only father she'd ever known. Papa Larry had no idea when he married Jean that her depression caused fits of rage.

Chapter Three: The story of Mom sitting in the hospital with me, a newborn. I was six weeks old when I mysteriously stopped breathing and was rushed to the hospital ICU. A doctor told Mom the lack of oxygen might cause brain damage.

Chapter Four: The story of my wedding day with Ron. As I walked down the aisle with Dad at my side, I cringed at the fact that neither Janie nor Nammaw Jean was there. Janie joined the military to find herself; the military dictated whether or not she could attend her sister's wedding. Nammaw Jean spent the day in bed, unable to get out of her pajamas or feed herself.

The remaining chapters wove each of these narrative stories into a single, cohesive theme: Women and their pain.

"It's the best book I've ever read," Mom said after I'd completed it. "Once I started reading, I couldn't stop."

I finished writing in time to print up the whole thing, slide it into a three-ring binder, and present it to Mom for Mother's Day.

"I wouldn't change a thing," she said as we sipped lemonade at a restaurant. "I wouldn't even change the names."

That was the book I shopped around to one-hundred different agents. Some responded with interest. One agent asked me to send her the entire manuscript. Six months later, she wrote back. "This is a great story, but it just doesn't fit in with our publishing needs at this time."

What? Had the story been too real, too painful? Discouraged, I slid the printed manuscript under my bed with the cobwebs.

I called Mom.

"Can you believe that Hailey asked me to lead MOPS?" I asked, not waiting for Mom to say hello. "Doesn't Hailey know that I'm a writer who has hearing loss? I mean, I can hardly stand on a stage and talk into a microphone because I barely hear myself talk. And she expects me to lead these MOPS meetings twice a month, and make phone calls to moms, and train all the other leaders, and lead prayers and service projects and bake sales and..."

"But Shanna..."

"And I have to explain to all these mothers how hard it is for me to hear them and keep reminding them to speak up and face me because — hello! — I am a lip-reader. Don't they realize that..."

"Whoa," Mom interrupted. "Let me talk without butting in."

"Fine."

"Remember those times I had to work weekends. You got yourself dressed and ready for church. Either Dad or someone from church would take you."

"Yeah, I guess."

"You went to church by yourself. No one told you to, but you did it."

"Okay."

"Do you remember that Bible I got you? Do you still even have it?"

I gazed at the worn leather-bound book in front of me, opened to 1 Corinthians.

"I bought that for you because you kept begging for it," Mom said. "You wanted to learn as much as you could so you'd be ready for church come Sunday. Do you remember that?"

I took in a deep breath, held it in. Then I let it hiss out like a dying balloon.

"And do you remember," Mom said, "how important reading that Bible was to you? Every morning, I'd find you in your room with your nose in that book. You had a pink highlighter, and I'd watch you underline verses you'd just read. Do you still even do that?"

I lay my Bible on the floor. The verses I had read in 1 Corinthians, chapter 13, were the same verses recited at my wedding: "Love is patient. Love is kind. It does not envy, it does not boast, it is not proud."

I'd underlined those verses, plus the ones below. "When I was a child, I talked like a child. I thought like a child, I reasoned like a child. When I became a man, I put childish ways behind me."

The next verse, number 12, was the part about seeing a poor reflection in a mirror, but eventually seeing things fully. I had bracketed that verse before calling Mom, and I'd written the day's date beside the words.

"Who's not to say God has brought you through everything you've gone through in order to prepare you for that MOPS stage," Mom said.

My next phone call was to Hannah. She was the friend who went to church with me on those Sundays when Mom had to work. Hannah was there with me the Saturday night, when at age fourteen, I had walked the aisle at a church revival. She held my hand as I prayed with a pastor to dedicate my life to the Lord.

"Hannah," I said into the receiver.

"How's it going?" she said.

"I need you to pray. Hard."

"About what?" Hannah said.

"I am about to do something I never planned on doing. I'm scared. But I think it's what I'm supposed to do."

"Okay, what is it?"

I let out a deep breath.

"I'm going to dedicate my life to God," I said. "Again."

The microphone on the church stage squealed as I spoke into it. Even with my hearing loss, I heard the audible gasp from the sixty moms sitting in the audience.

"Welcome to a new year of MOPS," I said, clutching the microphone stand. "I am Shanna."

After three months of training with Hailey on the importance of prayer, service, encouragement, and building my MOPS steering team, it was time to take the stage. I was now officially my church's MOPS leader.

"Do you know what MOPS stands for?" I asked.

Hands shot up.

"It's Mothers of Preschoolers, right?" asked a young woman on the front row. I squinted to lip-read her.

"Right. But do you know what it's all about?"

More hands were raised. Other answers were shouted out, words that I could barely hear or understand, despite using my best lip-reading ability.

This was going to be a long morning.

Most of these moms were new to MOPS and didn't have a clue who I was. Most of them hadn't seen me waltz around the stage several months earlier, the princess, singing about her hearing aids.

My wheat-colored hair hung limp in my face.

"Does anyone have a rubber band?"

Patricia, my friend who had the stroke, waved a rubber band with her healthy hand. I stepped off the stage toward her table.

"Thanks," I whispered, twisting the rubber band into my limp strands, pulling them away from my face.

"Without this ponytail, I'm just like all of you," I said as I returned to the stage. "But when I show you this..." I reached for the oatmeal-colored device resting behind my right ear. I held the device high into the air. "When I show you this — my hearing aid — you know that I am different. I am a different kind of mom. So is Patricia."

I pointed to my friend. "Patricia and I are two moms who have something that's hard for me to say. A disability. Does that mean we're bad moms — because she can't use one of her hands and I have hearing loss?"

I waved for Patricia to join me on the stage. She was eight months' pregnant with her third child. With the pregnancy weight she gained, Patricia needed two people to help her out of her chair. One of them carried her chair to the foot of the stage. The other led Patricia by the hand to the empty chair, where she could sit close to me.

"Everyone, say 'hi' to my friend, Patricia," I said.

I scanned the crowd of moms. Many of them wore beautiful necklaces and faces full of makeup. They wore fashionable blouses. Some of them had fresh manicures. I could see all of that from the stage, as well as the tears that formed in most of their eyes.

"Patricia had a stroke after her youngest child was born," I said. "I was diagnosed with hearing loss two months after my oldest son was born. We aren't perfect, but we're still MOPS.

Just like all of you."

As I put my hearing aid back in my ear, the moms rose to give Patricia and me a standing ovation.

The local newspaper received a tip that my MOPS group had adopted the Martinez family.

We planned an outing for Miguel's seven girls to a local T-shirt tie-dying store. Each mom chose a girl, offered to pay for her shirt and help her decorate it. The girls could wear their shirts to school and church. Clothing and our presence were the two best gifts we knew how to give.

Tia, the three-year-old girl, pointed at my ear.

It was a balmy July afternoon, and I had rushed to the tie-dye store after one of Nicklaus' T-ball games. Sweat beads formed on my forehead. In an attempt to cool down, I had yanked my hair out of my face and twisted it into a ponytail.

Tia touched my hearing aid.

"What that?" she said.

When I had given the MOPS presentation dressed as a princess, the subject of my speech was trust. For days, I wrestled with words that helped define trust. I finally came up with an acronym... T - To, R - Remove, U - Uncertainty, S - Seek, T - Truth.

These words fit my hearing-loss story. I had kept my hearing aids hidden beneath a layer of hair. In order to fully disclose my story, I had to lift that hair out of the way — remove that wall that kept me living in denial. Once the uncertainty was lifted, the truth could be sought. Revealed.

I typed the acronym onto a handout that was distributed

during my "I Am a Princess" speech.

Now I kneeled before Tia and forced a smile across my tight lips. With a free hand, I yanked one of the digital devices out of my ear. I cupped it in my hand so Tia could see.

"That's my hearing aid," I said to her. "My ears are broken. This helps my ears work better."

Defining state-of-the-art ear technology to a preschooler was a challenge — one that I practiced with Nicklaus. One time, he took the tires off his toy truck. Later I noticed black rubber objects dangling from his ears. "My hear aids." Nicklaus grinned, proud of his newfound contraptions.

Tia tilted her head to inspect the other hearing aid still tucked nice and neat behind my ear. Then she glared at the aid in my hand. Inquisitive was the word that described Tia and Nicklaus. At the age of three or four, a child found her voice. It was the way a preschooler found out things — to open her mouth and ask questions.

"Ms. Groves."

I felt a gentle tap on my shoulder.

A man with vintage wire-framed glasses met my gaze.

"I'm Alex from the paper," He held out his hand for me to shake. "Care if I ask you a few questions?"

As I shook Alex's hand, I noticed the enormous camera hanging from his neck.

"Sure."

Alex and I walked out of the tie-dye store into an open seating area inside the shopping mall. He sat and lifted his camera strap off his neck.

"Is this quiet enough for you?" he inadvertently stared at my ears.

My hearing aids were now on stage, a bright mall spotlight

beaming down on them. My true identity was revealed. I no longer was Shanna Groves. I was Ms. Hearing Aids.

Alex fired off a string of questions.

"How did you meet the Martinez family?"

"What do you know about the family?"

"How did your MOPS group get involved with the family?"

"What's it been like helping the family?"

Each time Alex said "the family," I wondered if he really wanted to ask me about "the hearing aids." Maybe his interview about the Martinez family was a ploy to get the inside scoop on my hearing loss. As much as he glared at my hardened oatmeal-colored hearing devices, I wondered when the question about my deafness would come up.

After taking front and side profiles of my face, I waited for Alex to spew out a final question.

"I guess that's it," he said, wrapping the camera strap around his neck.

Huh?

"I'll interview the other moms and talk to Mr. Martinez," Alex said. As he shook my hand for the final time, I noticed something about him that hadn't been clear to me before. Alex's eyeglasses were thick as soda-bottle glass.

Maybe his eyes hadn't detected my hearing aids after all.

I woke up with an uneasy feeling that it was going to be one of those days. I'd had that feeling before.

When I was pregnant with Reagan, I'd forced my eyelids open most days. The pillow was my favorite companion then. The more I slept, the more I could dream away the cobwebs that still lingered in my brain.

A few weeks before, I had stopped taking Happy Pills. The doctor and I agreed that I was well enough to wean myself off antidepressants. I started seeing a counselor, who offered emotional help that didn't come in the form of a chalky pill. During counseling, I dealt with the cobwebs still lurking in my thoughts. I was plagued with uncertainty about my hearing loss and how it would impact my future.

Someday I would likely return to an eight-to-five job. Nicklaus and Reagan would begin school. I couldn't stay at home, twiddling my antsy thumbs.

"What did you enjoy about work?" my counselor asked at our last session.

"The people. The conversation."

Counselor jotted notes on a legal pad in her lap.

"Do you think," she said, "that hearing loss will make it hard to work?"

That was the question keeping me awake at night and barely able to pry my eyes open during the day.

I lay in bed at nine o'clock on a Thursday morning. Nicklaus and Reagan remained in their bedrooms, in their pajamas and unfed.

The phone rang, but I didn't hear it. It was a high-pitched ring that my ears — without hearing aids in them — couldn't detect.

The answering machine clicked on. Its volume was cranked loud enough for me to hear.

"Shanna," the caller said. "It's Mom. If you're there, I need you to pick up."

The tone of Mom's voice through the amplified answering machine sounded serious. I had heard that same tone when she called to announce Nammaw Jean was dying.

I darted out of bed and whisked up the phone.

"Hello?" I said, out of breath.

"Shanna?"

"Yeah..."

"It's your dad."

"What about Dad?" I struggled to catch my breath.

"Shanna," she said. "Your dad had a heart attack. He's in the hospital. He's about to have surgery."

Mom's sentences were calm and staccato. They had a steady rhythm to them. Her voice was too calm.

"What happened...I mean, is he okay? When's his surgery? Do you know if..."

"Whoa," Mom said. "I think he'll be fine. It's just, I wanted you to know about the surgery. In case something..."

"I'm coming," I interrupted.

"What do you mean, you're coming?"

"I'll make the drive. I'll be there tonight."

"But the kids, you can't just..."

"Oh, I'll be there. If Ron has to take off work to watch them, I'm coming."

"But you'll miss the surgery," Mom said. "It's this afternoon."

I took a deep breath, the first one taken since the conversation began. "I don't care. I'm coming."

Dad came from a long line of heart problems. His father, my Grandpa Bartlett, died of heart disease. Grandpa Bartlett's father had heart issues.

The whole side of my Dad's family had some form of health issue — heart conditions, diabetes, even deafness.

As I drove my silver compact Honda on the two-lane

blacktop leading to the Oklahoma border, I thought about Dad's family. The Bartletts. They were my namesake before I married. My middle name, Delene, was a variation of Grandma Bartlett's name, Shirlene. The sky blue eyes, fair skin, and hundreds of moles that dotted my skin came from the Bartletts and their Irish ancestry.

Hearing loss, I found out after my diagnosis, ran rampant in the Bartlett family. I grew up listening to tales about this family I hardly knew.

The story about hearing loss in the Bartlett family was no secret. My parents took us to visit Grandpa and Grandma Bartlett once, maybe twice a year. During the few times I visited my grandparents, I sensed something was wrong with Grandpa Bartlett's hearing. His rotary phone that hung on the wall of his dilapidated farm house had an amplified ring. When someone called, the phone rang loud enough to wake me as I dozed in the guest room.

Once when the phone rang, Grandma Bartlett asked me to pick up the receiver. She was busy in the kitchen, and Grandpa dozed in his worn recliner.

"Hello?" I'd answered.

The caller's voice blared through the amplified phone's receiver. Deafening.

"Hold it away from your head," Grandma Bartlett hollered from the kitchen.

I held the phone a foot away from my ear and heard the caller's voice crystal clear.

Dad later explained that hearing loss had touched one of his brothers and one of his sisters. He said that my Uncle Sammy was born almost deaf. My Aunt Bernice started going deaf as a kid. Uncle Sammy had a son who was deaf, and Aunt

Bernice raised a son who was profoundly hard of hearing.

As Dad explained this all to me as a child, I half listened. It wasn't until driving to Oklahoma to be with my Dad now that his words fully sank in. Just as he had a family history of heart problems, I was part of a generational legacy of hearing loss.

Coffeyville, Kansas, was the last town before hitting the Oklahoma border. A rare August thunderstorm pummeled my Honda as I drove. Darkened clouds hovered in the sky like a flock of blackbirds. My visibility was less than fifty feet in front of my car.

To keep me company on the monotonous drive, I checked out an audio book from the library. It had been a couple of years since I attempted to listen to a book on tape. My hearing loss made the task laborious.

I struggled to hear the words of Rev. Billy Graham through the car's stereo speakers.

"God uses whatever means necessary to protect His children," the narrator spoke. At least, that's what I heard. Drops of rain splattered my windshield and the wind howled outside, competing with the words. What I thought I heard was that, like the enormous set of clouds lining the sky above, God hovered over me in my tiny Honda, providing His protection.

It reminded me of a phone conversation once with Hannah. She quoted to me from Psalm 91: "If you make the Most High your dwelling — even the Lord, who is my refuge — then no harm will befall you, no disaster will come near your tent."

The recorded book blared through my speakers. I read Billy Graham's news columns for years and was fascinated he had been preaching about God longer than my parents had been alive. With his piercing eyes and pointy chin, Graham reminded me of Grandpa Bartlett, who had preached in a country church before I was born.

The town of Coffeyville was desolate on the night my little car entered, driving through a blinding thunderstorm, while I listened to Graham's garbled words. It was one thing to have hearing loss and struggle to hear everything around me, but to be nearly blinded by rain on top of that?

The road, the town, everything I saw within my limited view was shrouded in the storm's dark rage. The only thing providing comfort was the sound of my audiotape talking about God this and Jesus that — the occasional words I understood.

As I crossed the town's main intersection, the one color I saw besides black night was the reflection of fiery red. A light shone onto my windshield from something that appeared to be above my hood. I didn't know what caused the glow until my headlights shined onto a rain-soaked wooden crossing.

Out my left window, I saw a train coming toward me.

Faster than my wipers swished, I shifted the car in reverse and slammed the gas pedal. "C'mon, c'mon," I pleaded with my Honda. "Don't fail me now."

As the car flew back, the faint glow of red in my windshield suddenly sharpened into view. A limp flashing red crossbar, broken in half, flashed in front of me. It looked as if it had hit something hard.

As the train proceeded to race behind that bar, out of my right window, my headlights revealed another moving object. I saw a man wearing overalls walk out of the darkness and onto the train track. He waved his arms overhead at the train's approaching engine. The train seemed to slow down.

On the train car was a platform and railing. Mystery Man reached for a bar and pulled himself onto the train. After that, I couldn't see him.

The train picked up pace and was out of view within a few minutes. Mystery Man and the train that nearly hit me fled town while I struggled to make sense of what I just saw.

We've all heard that things happen for a reason. That night, I knew what I had just witnessed happened for a reason.

All weekend while with my parents, I wrestled with images from my near collision. I also wrestled with thoughts of what could have happened if I hadn't backed up the car.

What stumped me was the broken railway crossbar. How had it been able to flash over me if it had been snapped in two? And what had that crossbar hit to cause its break?

With Dad on the mend but my thoughts still rattled, I made the drive home on Sunday. The sky was cloudless blue, warmed by the afternoon breeze.

As I approached Coffeyville, I saw the train crossing a half-mile away. It cut across the road in a diagonal and divided the roadway awkwardly in half. The crossbars seemed too close to the crossing, and I searched for the broken bar that had startled me just as much as that moving train.

Without a locomotive in sight, I approached the crossing and looked for that crossbar. A few feet away, it stood straight in the air, not a break on it.

I reached for the case of the Billy Graham audio book. I remembered the glowing red light, the train piercing through darkness, and Mystery Man waving his arms.

The title on the case, which I hadn't paid much attention to before, nearly caused me to skid off the road.

The book's title was *Angels*.

Had that man been an angel — or was I losing my mind?

14 A Life-Changing Phone Call

Confession: I love to hate telephones.

My nose pressed into the worn leather book Mom bought me almost twenty years before. I had become obsessed with this Bible since my close call with the train. I prayed over it, cried into it, even clutched it as I napped.

In my journal, I even had an acronym for it. B - Basic, I - Instructions, B - Before, L - Leaving, E - Earth.

The Mystery Man, who'd disappeared with the train, caused me to question. Was I supposed to live longer for a reason — a higher purpose? What would have happened had that train rammed into my Honda? How could my kids carry on without their mother, or Ron without his wife?

How much time did I have left on this earth?

I spilled out my story to anyone who would listen. At a MOPS leader meeting, I gathered a dozen of my mom friends together and told them about the stormy night and the man with the waving arms. They listened intently.

I told Mom and Dad when I visited that a train nearly struck my car, but that, miraculously, I lived to tell the story. Mom's response: "You need to drive more careful."

I managed to call Janie on her new boyfriend's cell phone.

She had returned to Oklahoma and had set up house in a mint-condition trailer home on the outskirts of Tulsa. She also promised my parents she would remain clean and sober. Janie had to stay sober; she'd just enlisted in the Army National Guard.

"Can you believe it?" I said as I told her my train story.

Janie didn't say anything for a moment. Just the word, "Wow."

Her voice was scratchy and hollow, as if she had been crying.

"Are you okay?" I asked.

The receiver filled with the sound of Janie's deep breath and sniffles. We hadn't talked much in the past few months, and I hadn't seen Janie at all since her three daughters had been taken out of the home by child-protective services. That was almost two years ago. This was the first time in a long time that Janie had a reliable phone number or a permanent address.

"I miss them." Janie's voice was a barely audible whisper.

I cranked up the volume switch on my amplified phone to hear her. "What was that?"

"I haven't seen my girls in so long. I just..." Janie sobbed.

"It'll be alright." I repeated this to Janie multiple times, long enough for her to gain composure.

"What have I done?" Again, Janie's voice was a whisper.

"What have you WHAT?" I asked.

"I chose drugs instead of my girls. What have I done?"

All I could do was sit silently, the phone clutched to my ear. I didn't have an answer for Janie.

I called Hannah.

"I'm so worried about Janie," I said when she answered.

Hannah, who enjoyed a lengthy phone chat on most occasions, was more succinct and to the point with me now.

Her words: "Go read Psalm 91."

After the shortest conversation with Hannah in the history of our friendship, I did as she said. I picked up my worn Bible, opened it in the center, and found the book of Psalms on my first try.

I shifted a few pages over to Psalm 91. As I scanned the words, I spotted the verses I had remembered when driving through Coffeyville, Kansas, to be with Dad.

"If you make the Most High your dwelling — even the Lord, who is my refuge — then no harm will befall you, no disaster will come near your tent."

The only people I ever knew who lived in a tent were my Dad's family, the Bartletts. The next two verses hadn't caught my eye until now.

"For He will command His angels concerning you to guard you in all your ways; they will lift you up in their hands, so that you will not strike your foot against a stone."

I was convinced an angel had visited me on that train crossing in Coffeyville. I was convinced my life had been spared.

I lay my face into the open Bible and sobbed.

"God," I cried, "please save my sister."

⌒

It was a frigid Thursday morning when the phone rang. I was two minutes from heading out the door with Nicklaus and Reagan to a play date.

"Hey Shan," I heard when I picked up the receiver. "It's Janie."

Her voice was less subdued than the last time we'd talk. In fact, she sounded a bit upbeat.

"Oh, hi." I sat on the kitchen floor, struggling to get Reagan's snow boot on her foot. "How are you?"

"Good, I guess," Janie said. "Hey, did you talk to Mom yet?"

I slid the other boot on Reagan's foot. "No. What's up?"

"I may be heading to Afghanistan."

Had I heard her correctly? Afghanistan was where Osama bin Laden, the mastermind of 9/11, lived.

"What?"

"My unit is on standby to deploy there, but it won't be for several months."

I waved Reagan on so she wouldn't see the look of horror in my eyes.

"How...what...How does Mom feel about this?"

"I don't know," Janie said. "Guess she's a little nervous."

A little nervous? I bet Mom was terrified, sending her youngest child into the land where terrorists lurked.

"How do you feel about this, Janie?"

"I'm okay. Actually, I'm curious about what's going on over there."

After two years of transient living and months wasted on drugs, Janie was finally back on her feet. No one was going to send my sister — my Baby Sister — into the wild to get shot at.

"We need to get together. Soon."

"Okay," Janie said.

"I'm driving through Tulsa next week. It's right on my way to see Mom and Dad. How 'bout I meet you somewhere for lunch? You can see Nicklaus and Reagan. She was four months old last time you saw her."

"Okay."

"You sure you can meet us?"

"If I don't have to work," Janie said.

"Good. We need to talk some more about this...Afghanistan."

The next day and a half were filled with odd errands. I drove all over town shopping and getting things ready for the visit to my parents. It was the first time we'd seen each other since Dad's heart scare hospitalization. Mom said he had his energy back. He would need it to keep up with my two kids.

I was in the car when my cell phone vibrated in my back pocket. It had become a habit to wear my cell phone so that I could feel it. Even with hearing aids in, my ears no longer could hear the phone ring.

It was Lydia, my sister. We talked sparingly, so I knew something was up.

"What's up?" I answered.

"Have you talked to the husband?" Lydia's voice was slow, each of the words clearly enunciated.

"I talk to 'my husband' a lot."

"Have you talked to him this afternoon? He's supposed to call you."

How in the world would Lydia know when Ron was supposed to call? The two spoke to one another by phone maybe once every three years. Thus, the reason for Lydia's affectionate term for him, "the husband."

"Uh...no," I said. "I'm out running errands." What type of stunt was Lydia trying to pull?

"Shanna, listen to me. I need you to drive home right now."

"What are you up to?"

"Just go home now. Ron will be there waiting for you."

"What? Did something happen?"

Lydia hung up.

What was that all about? The only times I heard from Lydia were if she had a problem, she had some family gossip to spout off or if she were coming to visit — which was rare.

Her words and tone of voice were much more to the point than normal. And why was Ron meeting me at home?

Most husbands only came home from work early to wait for their wives if it was Valentine's Day, an anniversary, or birthday. None of the above, in my case.

My fingers suddenly turned sweaty as I gripped the steering wheel and pressed my foot on the gas pedal.

When I got home, Ron sent the kids to watch a movie in the basement.

I rubbed my sweaty palms on my jeans. "What happened?"

Ron had that look in his eyes that shouted trouble.

"What happened? Is someone sick?" I said. "Did someone get hurt?"

"Shanna..."

"Is it Dad?"

Ron shook his head.

"Mom?"

"It's not your Mom, Shanna."

I saw a hint of wetness in his green eyes as they shifted from looking at the floor to looking at me.

"It's Janie."

I clenched my hands into fists. "What about Janie?"

"She's gone."

Gone where? On another road trip with her friends? To Afghanistan with her unit? She'd been called up early — that's what it was.

Ron sat next to me, his face a foot from mine. He grabbed one of my fists.

"Janie passed away in her sleep last night."

I smelled garlic on Ron's breath from something he had eaten at lunch. I pulled my fist out of his hand and pushed him away.

"Your breath stinks," I hissed at him.

"Shanna?"

"What? I just talked to her, and now you're telling me she's..." I stood up.

"I'm so sorry."

My words spewed out, like a bark. "So what happened?"

"The police who found her...They don't know."

"The police?"

"A friend went to wake Janie up this morning. But she wouldn't wake up. The friend must've called the police. They called your parents, and they called Lydia."

"So, why didn't they call me?"

"They didn't want to upset..."

"Upset me? Uh-huh. That's a good theory."

Ron walked over toward me, reaching his arms out.

"Come here," he said softly.

I pushed him again. "Just get away from me."

I ran up to my bedroom, slammed the door, and plopped on the bed. On the floor were my Bible and the black-speckled composition book I used as my journal. I picked them up and slammed them on the mattress. My fingers raced across the pages of my Bible, not settling on any page. I threw it back on the floor.

I opened to the back of my journal where four sheets of white paper remained. I had scribbled random thoughts, Bible verses, and memories of dreams into this particular journal nine months before. I had recorded the story of Reagan's second birthday party in it, my trip through Coffeyville, Kansas, with the angel at the train crossing. I had written down Bible verses from Genesis through Revelation in this book — verses that spoke to me during whatever I was experiencing at the time.

My last journal entry was dated January 25. It was a verse from Psalm 129.

"They have greatly oppressed me from my youth — let Israel say — they have greatly oppressed me from my youth, but they have not gained the victory over me."

Oh, God! Why? Why did you take her? Why did you take Janie? Why?

I had to call Mom and Dad, but I didn't want to. I didn't want to hear their desperate voices or listen to their cries. I didn't want to be the one to comfort them. I couldn't be the one.

I had to. I picked up my cell phone and dialed them.

Once the phone answered, all I heard was loud breathing on the other end.

"Hello?" I said.

I heard an exhausted, "Yeah?" Mom's voice.

"Oh, Mom."

"Yeah?"

"Mom, I..."

"Uh-huh."

"I, just...oh, Mom..."

Neither of us said anything but 'Yeah' and 'Oh' for the next several seconds.

"I'm afraid..." Mom's voice trailed off.

I closed my eyes. "What are you afraid of?"

Mom let out a few more raspy breaths.

"That..."

"What Mom?"

"That I'll never recover from losing my child."

I dropped the phone into my lap and banged my fist into the open pages of my journal.

⁓

In five days, I lost five pounds.

After the phone call with Mom and Dad, I spoke with close friends and a minister from my church. As soon as I hung up the phone, it would ring again. Ron got the kids to bed early so I could pack for the drive the next day to be with my parents.

Day one of the visit: Lydia and I met at a McDonald's off the Kansas turnpike, a half-way spot for both of us. Ron and the kids drove me to meet Lydia, then they turned around and went home. We decided my parents didn't need kids running around the house while planning their daughter's funeral.

Day two: Lydia, Dad, and I drove to meet with the director of the small-town funeral home. Mom wouldn't get out of bed that morning. The three of us agreed on a pink casket with an extravagant price tag.

Day three: Lydia and I drove to the shopping mall to find Janie's burial outfit. The director had told us to pick something with a high-collar since Janie's body had undergone an autopsy; the results wouldn't be back for a month. Lydia and I selected a dusty rose turtleneck with matching suit jacket and ankle-length skirt. Lydia purchased a cross necklace to go with the outfit.

Day four: Lydia insisted on doing Janie's hair and makeup for the service. No one could convince her otherwise. While Lydia drove into town to purchase cosmetics, I stayed behind with Mom, Dad, and their entourage of visitors. Dad's brother, my uncle Sammy Bartlett came, as did Aunt Bernice and her husband. Since neither had seen me since I was twelve, they had little idea of my hearing loss or that I wore hearing aids. While we chitchatted in the living room over iced tea, I took off my hearing aids and displayed them to everyone as if it were show-and-tell time. Aunt Bernice showed me her pair — twice the size of my own. Uncle Sammy didn't wear hearing aids. He preferred to lip read only. It was a bittersweet reunion for the Bartletts.

Day five: I got up early to glean all the photos of Janie I could find in my parent's house. We wanted to put together a memory board to be displayed next to her casket. Dad pulled out dusty boxes from the attic filled with high school trophies, news clippings, and albums. One box had several letters tucked inside — some from old boyfriends, some from Nammaw Jean to me when I was in college, a couple written by Janie. Lydia and I lay on my childhood bed with the attic contents spread about, laughing about silly things we collected when we were kids. I found sixteen photos of Janie for the memory board.

Day six: Ron and the kids were staying at my in-laws, an hour away from my parents. He planned to drive in before the funeral service to meet with the rest of the family. Lydia and I argued about the venue for Janie's service. Lydia wanted a location large enough to accommodate anyone who came. Dad and I agreed that our childhood church was where we should say good-bye to Janie. The tiny country church was a mile off the main road in town. At capacity, the building could accommodate no more than a hundred people. As friends from high school, neighbors, and relatives packed into the church, everyone knew this service would be standing room only.

Some visitors waited in the lobby, unable to find a place to sit. Others stood in the fellowship hall behind the main building. It was too cold and rainy to force the overflow of people outside. The gravel parking lot turned into a giant mud pie, with car tires spinning in pot holes as they attempted to park.

Pastor Clearthroat knew my family by name only. My parents hadn't regularly attended church since Janie and I were still at home. When he stood at the pulpit to recognize the family, he pronounced both mine and Lydia's names wrong.

When he made the faux pas, Lydia glanced at me. My stomach, filled with butterflies of anxiety for the past five days, suddenly relaxed. I covered my face with a hand, slid down in my pew, and let out a nervous snicker. I wanted to scream at him, "My name is Shanna, not Shawna!"

"And now," the pastor announced, "one of the members of the family would like to share a few words."

I glanced at Lydia.

"Go," she mouthed, pointing to the pulpit.

The eulogy. It was like a repeat of Nammaw Jean's funeral with no one wanting to deliver a eulogy and me feeling guilty if I didn't do it. I let go of Ron's hand and stood.

Pastor Clearthroat held the microphone out for me as I walked down the aisle. I passed several people I hadn't seen since childhood.

When I grabbed hold of the microphone, I saw a row of people standing along the church's back wall. One of those people was Becky, my MOPS friend who had driven five hours to be there.

The words to Janie's eulogy were written down, but I didn't

need them. They had been memorized long ago.

I told the Goodnight Prayer.

"Goodnight."

"Goodnight," Janie would repeat.

"I love you."

"I love you, too."

"Forever."

Forever," Janie repeated.

"No matter what we do."

"No matter what we do."

I gazed at the audience. Ron's head was bowed. Mom's head was buried in Dad's shoulder. Lydia looked at me, stone-faced. Janie's ex-husband sat in the row behind them, alone, staring at the floor.

"And then at this part of the prayer," I said, "is when things got silly."

I rattled off all the names of movie stars, teen heartthrobs, and cartoon characters we loved as kids.

"I love..."

"I love," Janie would repeat.

"Kirk Cameron."

"Corey Haim."

"Corey Feldman."

"Corey Feldman?" I'd ask. "Ewwwww..."

Laughter trickled through the church.

"As long as I live," I said, "as long as I breathe. Every night when I go to bed, I will say that prayer to Janie."

After I walked away from the pulpit and slid back into my pew, I bowed my head.

A few days after Janie died, as Ron and I lay in bed, I confessed to him some of my regrets. What if I had called her more often? What if I had made better efforts to see her? What if she hadn't died — would we be able to have our lunch together?

My mind reeled with the fact that Janie died a few days before we planned to meet in Tulsa. She had suggested the casino near her trailer house, which had an all-you-can-eat-buffet to die for. Her words.

Janie's autopsy results came back. Cause of death: drug toxicity. I hadn't wanted to know more about those drugs in her system, but Mom told me anyway. OxyContin. An anti-depressant of some name I couldn't remember. An over-the-counter antacid medicine — all medications taken for pain.

March 10

> *I woke up today and knew that things were going to be different. They had to be.*
>
> *Yesterday was the one-month anniversary of Janie's death. I don't remember ever feeling more brokenhearted. I dreaded when the time came for me to finally cry. Yet, as I pictured her 29-year-old face in my mind, I realized she would never turn 30. There was no goodbye, no hug, no catching up over lost time.*
>
> *I didn't want to be alone in the days after her funeral because I was afraid to grieve. Afraid to feel all the weight of what had been lost. Afraid of sinking into the abyss of depression.*
>
> *Then the kids and I got sick with head colds and were forced to spend some time at home. The one-*

month anniversary approached, and I felt the hole of pain inside myself grow. There was no one who could put a bandage on this hole.

Nicklaus got well and returned to school on the day that marked four weeks since Janie had gone. Reagan and I still had our colds, and I put her in her crib to rest. I lay in my bed and tried to do the same.

I lay still and just let the memories — good and bad — wash over me like a thunderstorm. The hole of grief burst open, and all the pain spilled out in tidal waves of longing. I wanted Janie back. I prayed to Jesus and to her. I begged for one more chance.

I slammed my journal's cover and tossed it to the floor. The book was now full. Over the last few days as I hunkered down under the covers, trying to get well, unable to care for Nicklaus and Reagan or myself, I wrote my thoughts.

It was time to get up. The sun shone brightly through my blinds as I lifted the covers off the bed. After getting Reagan up from her nap and picking up Nicklaus from school, we drove five miles to a local park. It was the one with our favorite walking trail. A full year had passed since we last stepped on that path with its towering trees and nearby creek.

We got out and headed toward the paved walking path that paralleled the creek and row of trees. Nicklaus skipped several feet ahead while Reagan and I followed.

Reagan took a few steps forward before stopping to admire a broken twig on the ground. She'd take a few more steps and stopped to touch a rock on the pavement.

I called for Nicklaus to wait for us. He slowed down for a few seconds, then resumed his rapid-fire skipping. Reagan continued her much slower pace. She gazed up at the trees with their new spring flowers waiting to bud.

She walked toward a stick on the path and picked it up.

"Walk stick," she babbled.

I stopped to watch her with that stick. She waved it proudly in the air, as if it were her shining queen's scepter. The fluttering of newly grown tree leaves above us seemed to be clapping at her.

The breeze flew over us gently as we continued the walk. A familiar voice whispered to me, "Be still."

I recognized the words from the forty-sixth chapter of Psalms.

"Be still, and know that I am God."

15 Anointed in New Jersey

Confession: At higher altitudes, chew gum.

In the days after Janie's funeral, I noticed birds fluttering around me. A snow white bird wove in and out between parked cars at a café. I sat and gazed at it while eating a cinnamon crunch bagel.

A flock of blackbirds chased after each other at a field near an indoor playground where Nicklaus and Reagan chased each other. I watched the birds do their soaring dance above the stoplights.

February 15 was the date Janie and I had planned to meet for lunch at the casino outside of Tulsa. The day came and went without a meeting or a phone call from Janie. She was somewhere else — high above the birds and the clouds and the only earth I knew.

March 15 would have been Janie's thirtieth birthday. I scoured the greeting cards at a local store, hoping to find something that would convey my feelings for her. Where would I mail the card? As I drove home, I noticed gray geese flying overhead and wondered if these winged creatures were messengers. Was Janie safe and soaring even though I couldn't see her?

On the first day of spring, I stared out a window and noticed a flock of birds gliding below a couple of wispy clouds. It was windy and warm with humid air. January and early February stripped the trees bare in the bitter cold. Early signs of vegetation began to sprout.

Now, as Nicklaus and I sat on an airplane, I felt like those birds flying high above a blanket of clouds. Lights blinked above us, letting us know we could unfasten our seat belts.

Ron stayed home with Reagan while Nicklaus and I flew north to Janie's second memorial service. We didn't have the money for four plane tickets. Mom and Dad wanted the entire family at the service, including kids, since it had been planned by Janie's twin daughters, Callie and Cara. They lived with their father and hadn't been able to attend the funeral and burial in Oklahoma. A service would be a chance for the eight-year-old girls to say goodbye to their mother.

While the flight attendants announced something I couldn't hear over the loud speaker, I toyed with my seatbelt. Nicklaus babbled something I couldn't understand. He shouted to me, and I watched his lips move and his eyebrows furrow. I heard the roaring engines as we soared above the clouds — and nothing else.

Without the ability to hear, I'd once read, a person can lip-read about thirty-seven percent of what someone else says. My mind was too unfocused to lip-read Nicklaus. I couldn't concentrate on anything but thoughts of birds, clouds, and pain. My stomach muscles tightened with each mumbled overhead announcement. Was I missing key details about our flight?

We landed at the Newark airport outside of New York City.

"Shanna!"

Nicklaus and I were greeted with a familiar voice as we stepped out of the terminal.

"How was your flight?" Hannah said, taking Nicklaus' bag.

My friend pulled her fire engine red Suburban away from the curb. Her two young girls sat in the backseat — one with a head full of chocolate spiral curls and two front teeth missing, the other with a strawberry blonde bob and a thumb plopped in her mouth.

The last time I visited Hannah, we were pregnant with our first babies. My due date was a week ahead of Hannah's, and we both — at seven months' pregnant — wobbled down the streets of Manhattan on a sightseeing excursion. We rode the elevator to the top of the Empire State Building and saw the skyline of New York City. The Twin Towers stood erect in the distance. Less than a year later, they would crumble to the ground on 9/11.

"We hit the turnpike now, we'll make it to the 'o-tel' by midnight," Hannah said, steering us out of the Newark, New Jersey, airport parking lot. "Do we 'av' late check-in?"

"Huh?"

Hannah glanced at me. "At the o-tel' — do we av late check-in?"

Hannah had known me for so long, it was easy for her to forget that I had progressive hearing loss. It was one thing to chat with her a couple of times a month on my amplified phone with the volume control switch. In the car, with its rumbling motor and kids chatting in the backseat, I didn't understand my friend's words.

"I'm sorry, Hannah. But...can you repeat what you said?"

She shook her head. "Wow."

"What?"

She stared straight at me. "Can you hear me at all?"

I caught the "ear" part — at least I thought that's what she said. Something was wrong with my hearing aids. They amplified background noises more than Hannah's voice. I hadn't struggled this much since I first stepped foot in an audiologist's office six years ago.

Hannah flashed a cold stare into the rearview mirror.

"That'll be enough," she said to Nicklaus.

"What did he say?"

Hannah shook her head again.

"What?"

In a clear, enunciated voice and looking directly at me she said, "He called you 'stupid mom.'"

⁓

Giggling, screaming girls filled the hotel room.

"Pillow fight!" squealed Callie and Cara. My identical twin nieces looked like the same child. Their all-one-length golden hair nearly covered their round faces and ocean blue eyes. If they had been dressed alike, I wouldn't have known one from the other.

The twins bunked on the floor, while Hannah, her daughters and I shared the full-size beds. Nicklaus stayed next-door with Lydia and her son. Mom and Dad were the only ones resting comfortably in their private room two doors down.

My ears ached from the shrill excitement of little girls celebrating a hotel sleepover with their long-lost Aunt Shanna. I quickly yanked my hearing aids out, tucked them into their overnight case and kept them hidden in my purse under the bed, away from flying pillows.

"Aunt Shaaaa-naaaa," called Callie.

Born a couple of minutes before Cara, she took the role

of protective big sister seriously. Callie was the one who took care of Cara on the days when Janie wasn't sober — before child protective services sent them to live with their father.

"Whatcha' got in there?" Callie pointed to a couple of gift bags I had pulled out of my suitcase.

The week before, I went through Janie's belongings with Mom and Dad. They retrieved most of Janie's clothes, shoes, and purses from her trailer. Because we wore a similar size, they told me to pick whatever I wanted. Still hanging on a plastic hanger was the outfit Janie had intended to wear the next day. It was a carnation pink knit V-neck sweater that fell to the knees, along with a shimmery black ankle-length skirt. Janie's black leather jacket hung over the sweater. I snatched this outfit along with her nightgown, a few blouses, a pair of tennis shoes, and three purses.

One of the purses — a sequined saddle bag — I carried on the plane. The bag hadn't left my side in a week.

The other two purses were a clutch style and much too small for me — a mom of two — to carry all of my incidentals and my kids' stuff. The clutches were the perfect size for the girls.

I handed the girls the gift bags.

"Open them."

Callie opened hers first. It was a zebra-striped purse with hot pink accents. Cara's purse came in the same color scheme but in a more traditional striped pattern.

The day before Janie's funeral, my sister Lydia found an oval pearl-studded, palm-size frame. On the day Lydia did Janie's hair and makeup for the funeral, she tucked inside of the frame the only studio shot taken of Callie and Cara with their little sister, Annie. Each girl wore an Easter dress, and the backdrop featured an ethereal sky with clouds. They looked angelic. When the coffin closed, Janie's lifeless hands still cradled that framed photo.

Although I didn't have a copy of that photo, I had plenty of snapshots when Callie and Cara were babies. In one, Janie cradled her three-week-old twins at the baby shower hosted by the same country church ladies who later attended her funeral. In another shot, taken the week before the shower, Janie showed off her protruding stomach in its ninth month of pregnancy.

I placed each of these photos in an oval frame and slid one in each purse. Callie pulled out the pregnancy photo, while Cara gazed at the picture of Janie holding her and Callie.

"Keep these photos safe, girls," I said.

I'm not sure why I used the word "safe." Maybe it was the need to guard these items of Janie's. My sister's clothes, which hung in the basement closet at my house, remained on the same hangers and unworn — Janie's leather jacket, skirt, and blouse all with the aroma of Janie's hairspray and cigarette smoke still clinging to the cloth. Although a tad too big and not my style, I liked the way her clothes smelled.

Cara and Callie squeezed beside me on the bed. Their long legs stretched out onto the mattress, and we squeezed our pillows under our heads and lay there together. I stroked their hair.

～

Janie's memorial service was only the second time I had sat in a Catholic parish. Attending a Catholic service was nothing like my experience growing up in a Southern Baptist church. In my childhood, church congregants freely sang as loud as their voices would carry, while waving their hands and clapping to the instrumentals.

At the memorial service with Callie and Cara, the tone was subdued and silent. Even with my defective hearing aids, I heard Nicklaus' sneakers tap the hard wood floors.

When the priest spoke, I tuned him out. People filled two rows in the sanctuary. My family filled up an entire pew. The remaining visitors were presumably friends from Callie and Cara's church.

When the priest bowed and closed his eyes, the church friends knelt on a special padded stool directly beneath the pew in front of them. My family prayed like we always did — sitting on our rear ends.

The priest motioned to the girls. They stood with their father, walked past him, and followed each other to the pulpit. Callie held a folded piece of paper in one hand and Cara's hand with the other.

Callie leaned into the microphone. "My momma once took us to an amusement park."

At least, that's what my ears heard. I stared intently at Callie's lips, hoping for some understanding of what she said.

While the audience chuckled after Callie said something, I wondered what that something was. When the audience clutched their tissues to their faces, I wondered what Callie spoke that was so sad. I searched for any visual cues from Hannah, Lydia, Mom, or Dad as to what Callie's message was. Their heads faced forward, oblivious to my confused stares.

What was happening?

The ringing in my ears — an ever-present part of my hearing loss — intensified after Janie's death. My audiologist told me to avoid salt, caffeine and stress, which could increase the severity of tinnitus. I avoided soda and coffee for years, and salt wasn't a craving. But in the past month, I experienced near-debilitating stress.

At night, I slept intermittently. Back home, I was the last one to bed and the first one awake. When I wasn't chasing Nicklaus and Reagan around the house, I remained on my feet. Nervous energy propelled me to deep-scrub the house and bake two-dozen cupcakes two days after Janie's funeral. I threw myself into being a MOPS leader. Even though I couldn't sleep, I kept up with MOPS activities, only missing one meeting — the day of Janie's funeral. My mind raced with thoughts I couldn't reign in.

Now my ears reeled with unbearable tinnitus noise, which I hoped would have subsided once I got off the plane with Nicklaus. I'd chewed gum while in flight to keep altitude pressure from filling my ears with fluid. I'd chewed gum in the car with Hannah, in the hotel room with Callie and Cara, and now in church.

When Callie and Cara finished speaking and the priest recited a final prayer, I remained seated.

Hannah tapped my shoulder. "You coming, Shanna?"

Everyone else had their coats on, ready to leave.

My ears rang so loud, I couldn't hear myself respond with, "Yeah."

A rain shower followed us as we drove miles away from where Callie and Cara lived with their father. After the service and lunch with the girls, Hannah and I made the four-hour drive back to her house in New Jersey. The next day, we hoped to make it to Hannah's church for Sunday worship before driving into New York City. Mom and Dad had planned a day-long sightseeing outing with Lydia and her son, Callie, and Cara before Nicklaus' and my plane departed.

As we entered the town where Hannah lived, she slowed the car.

"Are you tired of having hearing loss?" she said, looking at me.

I watched Hannah's lips as she mouthed the words "tired" and "hearing loss" and put two-and-two together as to what she had asked.

"I hate it."

With our kids asleep in the backseat, Hannah turned the steering wheel to a shoulder on the side of the road and put the car in park.

Hannah turned her head so I could see her lips. "God doesn't want this for you."

"What...does he want, then?"

Hannah flashed her green eyes at me.

"God wants you to be whole, Shanna. He wants you to hear your kids. He wants you to hear when Nicklaus is calling you 'stupid mom' so that you can correct him. God wants you to hear."

"What do you want me to do?"

"What we can do," Hannah said, "is pray. Pray that this crushing hold that hearing loss has on you would be released. Pray that you would hear all that God wants you to hear."

"What do you mean...pray?"

Hannah grabbed one of my hands.

"The Bible says if you pray believing that you have received, without doubting, then you will receive it. Do you know what that means?"

I allowed Hannah's words to sink into my brain. I had lip-read the words "Bible," "pray," and "receive." And I knew

Hannah had asked me a question.

"I do read the Bible. I do pray..."

"For what?" Hannah asked, her voice sharp. "For the strength to make it through one more day of hearing loss? Is that really what God wants you to pray?"

I heard the words "strength" and "God."

"I do pray for God's strength," I said.

Hannah tightened her grip on my hand. "But do you pray for his healing?"

She enunciated each word so that I heard seven tiny sentences: "But. Do. You. Pray. For. His. Healing?"

How in the world would God heal my ears? I had progressive hearing loss. I was gradually becoming deaf. How could God possibly intervene? Hadn't the damage to my ears already been done?

I closed my eyes. "I don't think so."

Hannah touched her free hand to my face. "Look. At. Me."

When I opened my eyes, I noticed tears forming in Hannah's.

"We've got to pray for your healing," she said, tears sliding down her cheeks.

Some may be skeptical of the healing-prayer belief. I was. Doctors and medicine contribute to healing, but people who pray? In today's airbrushed, Photoshopped world, flaws can be erased in just a few keystrokes. My hearing loss was something I wanted to disappear. I was overwhelmed at any possibility that I wouldn't have to wear hearing aids to have a normal conversation, or that my children could ask me a question one time and I would understand them.

The next morning, Hannah and I slid into the pew at a nondenominational church in suburban New Jersey. We were fifteen minutes late, so we chose a pew toward the back.

Standing at the front was a pastor who resembled Sylvester Stallone dressed in his Sunday best. He looked more the part of a Hollywood stunt double for Rambo than a charismatic preacher.

As he spoke, I did something I normally did when attending church: zoned out. It was an impossible feat to lip read a man who barely opened his lips when he spoke and stood fifteen rows away from me.

Pastor Rambo pulled a peppermint out of his pants pocket, plopped it in his mouth, and continued preaching. With his left cheek bulged while he sucked on a mint, I gave up trying to interpret any words coming out of his sly mouth.

He motioned for the audience to stand, and Hannah tugged at my arm.

"This is it," she said, slowly. "Do you want to go pray?"

Her lips were so close to my face, I could smell the raisin bagel from breakfast on her breath. Not sure of how to answer, I nodded and stood.

Hannah grabbed my hand and led me to the altar. Pastor Rambo held a shiny flat Bible to his chest. His coal black eyes gazed into mine as I approached him.

"What can I pray with you about?" The pastor's voice was a low baritone, an easy tone for me to hear if I stood an inch from his stoic lips.

Hannah answered, "My friend is hard of hearing. We want to pray that her hearing loss would be lifted, that God would deliver her from progressive hearing loss."

"Is that so?" Pastor Rambo's eyes didn't blink as he gazed my way. "And how long have you dealt with this hearing loss?"

I wasn't sure what his question was or how to answer. "Um..."

"It's been six years," Hannah cut in.

"Six years." Pastor Rambo nodded. "Are you familiar with Scripture that talks about prayer for healing?"

"Well, um..."

"I am," Hannah said.

"And you?" The pastor nodded at me.

"Well, um, I guess..."

Pastor Rambo opened his Bible, flipping the pages a few times before stopping.

"The book of James," he read. "Is anyone of you sick? He should gather together with the elders of his church and pray for healing. The prayer offered in faith will make the sick person well. The Lord will raise him up.'"

I kept hearing the word "he" in reference to healing. Didn't the Bible include "she's"?

Pastor Rambo closed his Bible and tucked it under an arm. He reached into his coat pocket for what I thought would be another breath mint. Instead, he pulled out a small jar.

"Have you ever been anointed with oil?"

I shook my head. What in the world was he talking about?

"The Bible says that the elders are to anoint your forehead with oil when you pray for healing." He opened the jar's lid. "I'm going to do that now."

Had I agreed to this?

"Raise your hands, palm up, in honor of our Lord."

Robotically, I did as I was told. Hannah placed her hand on my shoulder.

"Close your eyes," he said.

For the next few seconds, Pastor Rambo prayed a pray I couldn't clearly hear. I caught some of his words: God, prayer, Jesus, heal. But I missed three-fourths of what he prayed.

I was so tired of lip-reading and not being able to understand. With my eyes closed, it was a no-win situation. I felt his fingertip wipe oil across my forehead. Then I felt gentle taps on my ears, one at a time.

The weight of not being able to hear him or my kids or any of the people I loved fell off my shoulders. All the stress I experienced from watching people's lips move, attempting to interpret what came out of them. All the shame of not hearing my son call me bad names from the back seat of the car. All the guilt at not hearing my kids cry from the other room if they were hurt or scared. The weight and the burden and the guilt poured out of me.

I wept.

When the prayer ended, I opened my eyes. The pastor motioned for me to remove my hearing aids, which I did. He then asked me to repeat what he said, without reading his lips.

Pastor Rambo covered his mouth and I heard, "What state do you live in?"

I answered him, and he and Hannah exchanged hopeful glances. I guess I'd answered correctly.

As we drove away from the New Jersey church, I closed my eyes and listened to the sounds. With the window cracked, I heard moving cars coming from the nearby highway. That sound had been deaf to my ears without hearing aids in them. Deep in my purse, I had buried those aids. I never wanted to wear them again.

"Idiot." It was a child's voice. "Stupid mom."

I opened my eyes and watched as Nicklaus, sitting beside me, spouted off these words. His tiny voice was not only audible to my ears, but annoying in its high pitch.

I grabbed hold of his arm.

"You listen to me," I said in my mean-mom voice. "I'd better never, ever hear you say that again. Do you understand?"

Nicklaus shook as I held his arm tight.

"That's right," Hannah added from the front seat. "You'd better listen to her."

I had heard my son with my eyes closed. From a distance and with her back facing me, I had understood Hannah's words without having lip-read her.

"I'm healed," I whispered to myself.

Hannah whipped her head around to face me.

"Yes, you are. Don't ever doubt God again," she whispered.

When we drove into Manhattan for an afternoon of family sightseeing, Hannah broke the news to Mom, Dad, and Lydia.

"So you can hear us, Shanna?" Mom walked several feet behind me as we strolled past Radio City Music Hall.

I turned around. "Loud and clear."

Mom suddenly stopped on the sidewalk while everyone else walked on. I stood beside her.

"You can hear me?" Mom spoke in an over-enunciated tone of voice. The obnoxious tone people often used with me so I could hear them well.

"Do me a favor," I said. "Quit using that voice."

Without my hearing aids in, I heard taxi cabs honking their horns. I heard my shoes shuffling on the sidewalk. I carried on a conversation with Mom without having to stop every few seconds to stare at her lips.

I had been healed. It was a miracle. I wasn't deaf anymore.

But was it real? I wanted documented proof that something had changed in my hearing ability. A week after the trip with Hannah, I headed to my audiologist's office.

"Good morning." A cheerful young woman behind the receptionist's desk greeted me. I'd never met her before.

It had been a couple of years since my ears had been tested. For someone with progressive hearing loss, changes in hearing ability can happen frequently. I'd been told by the doctor to come in for a hearing test one to two times a year or more.

"I'll be testing you today." The woman picked up a medical chart. "I'm Jeanette."

She looked directly at me as she spoke, her voice still cheerful. Jeanette appeared to be nineteen, maybe twenty years old.

"Are you an..."

"Yep, I'm an audiologist," she answered for me. "Don't look like one do I?"

I nodded. Jeanette led me to a room with a listening booth. I vaguely remembered the first time I had stepped in one of these contraptions. I had worn headphones and listened to a series of beeps and pushed a button every time I heard them. Sheer torture for my messed-up ears.

"Have a seat." She pointed to a leather chair. Next to it was a table, holding various hearing aid tweaking devices. A tool for cleaning ear wax out of hearing aid ear molds. A pocket-sized flashlight.

Jeanette picked up the flashlight. "Why don't you take your hearing aids out and we'll look in your ears."

"I don't have them in."

Jeanette's cheerful smile faded. "What?"

"Can you test me first, then I'll explain about my hearing aids?"

She lowered the flashlight on the table. "Yeah, I guess so."

Butterflies fluttered their dance inside my stomach as I entered the testing booth. Would I be able to hear all the beeps? Would I be able to understand all of Jeanette's words? Did she think I was crazy?

I placed the chunky headphones over my ears as she closed the booth's soundproof door. She sat in a chair outside the booth, which faced a soundproof window where we could see each other. A table with a computer, testing equipment, and a microphone sat beside her. She leaned into the microphone. The audio in my headphones crackled as she switched them on.

"Can you hear me?" Her voice was crystal clear through my headphones.

I gave her the thumbs up sign. As she proceeded with the testing, my body grew as rigid as a stone. I hunched in my seat, my fingers curled around the chair's armrests.

Beep.

I pushed the button.

Beep. Beep.

I pushed the button two times.

Low beep.

I pushed.

Mid-range beep.

Push.

A series of mid-range beeps.

Push. Push. Push.

My headphones were quiet. I closed my eyes and gritted my teeth, waiting for another beep — a higher tone beep — to be heard. It would be a higher frequency tone that my ears couldn't distinguish without hearing aids.

Beep.

What was that?

Beep. Beep.

I pushed the button two times.

Beep. Beep. Beep.

I pushed three times.

The next beep sounded like someone letting out a quick breath.

Push.

The headphones crackled again.

"Okay," Jeanette said through the microphone. "I'm going to say some words, and I want you to repeat them back to me."

She raised her hand to her lips to cover them so I wouldn't be tempted to lip-read.

"Bat."

"Bat," I repeated.

"Ball."

"Ball."

We went back and forth with our verbal exchange until the headphones became silent again. Jeanette opened the booth's door. In her hand was a sheet of paper with lines all over it. My hearing test results.

"Can you tell me what happened?" she said in a quiet voice.

I got up from my chair. "What do you mean?"

Jeanette waved the sheet of paper in front of me.

"This test shows you've gotten some hearing back."

I wasn't crazy. My ears could hear better. I now had proof of it.

"Well, if you want to know the whole story, it could take a while."

Jeanette handed me the test results, then plopped back in her seat.

The skin on her forehead bunched up in wrinkles as she raised her eyebrows high.

"I'm all ears," she said.

16 Peace, Love, and Hearing Loss

*Confession: If I could start all over again,
I'd only change my underwear.*

One morning, I woke up with better hearing than
the day before. I knew it was because of the healing
prayer in New Jersey, a bold act of faith for my usually dubious self.

Waking up with better hearing was like walking outside,
expecting a layer of snow on the ground, but instead finding daffodils and tulips bursting through the frozen turf with yellow joy.

Then one day, an ice storm tears through the flowerbed.
The early signs of spring couldn't fight off winter's return. The
foliage freezes. When the ground thaws, the once jubilant
flower petals drop to the wet mulch.

One month after the healing prayer, I woke up with a
clogged feeling in my right ear. It felt like a thin layer of cotton was wedged in the ear hole. I swabbed out the ear, but the
fluid remained. I tried to pop the ear pressure by yawning,
blowing my nose, and chewing gum. The next day and the
morning after that, the fluid remained.

Nicklaus and Reagan babbled words to me at breakfast,
and I pretended to hear them. I nodded and said, "Okay."

Ron leaned over that night to whisper sweet nothings in
my clogged right ear, and I faked a laugh and loving smile.

I couldn't hear out of my right ear.

To be hard of hearing, then not, then hard of hearing again was confusing. If God had wanted me whole again, why was that wholeness suddenly snatched away?

I tossed and turned at night, hoping the movement of my head would miraculously relieve the pressure in my right ear. When I couldn't sleep, I retreated to my journal.

April 20

It was the middle of the night and my right ear suddenly unclogged. I was so excited I woke up Ron and kissed him. I had trouble falling back to sleep but eventually did.

When Ron got up to leave for work at 7 a.m. I noticed my right ear was still unclogged but ringing loudly. After he left, I prayed the ringing would stop. While praying, my right ear clogged again.

"God," I prayed, "please unclog this ear for good."

I experienced so many emotions in just as many hours — elation, peace, confidence, burden, confusion, despair. Was I losing my mind?

April 21

This Saturday morning, Ron and I snuggled in bed. Nicklaus played with his action figures on our bedroom floor. The sun filtered through the window blinds. The high today is supposed to be 80. My right ear is still clogged.

A thought flitted through my brain: "Janie gave up

on life, right? Why don't I give up, too? Then I can be where she is."

April 23

   Ron and I took the kids to see the Disney animated film, "Meet the Robinsons." It starred an orphaned boy who took a time machine into the future. Instead of cars, the future was filled with flying bubbles. At the closing credits, a quote flashed across the screen:
   "Keep moving forward." -Walt Disney
   Sitting in the theater with Ron holding my hand, Nicklaus enraptured with the movie, and Reagan on my lap kissing and hugging me over and over, my feelings of confusion and sadness over the past week began to lessen.

~

I decided the only way to relieve my ear pressure was to see a doctor. Modern medicine had worked its magic when I suffered depression. Maybe it could restore my hearing.

The doctor prescribed gigantic amoxicillin tablets to take twice a day for ten days. Every time I swallowed a tablet, I closed my eyes and imagined the fluid in my ear gradually dissipating.

Days one through five: Right ear still clogged.

Days six through 10: Right ear still clogged.

With no relief, I headed to the doctor for yet another round of antibiotics. If amoxicillin couldn't gush out the fluid in my ear, maybe another miracle pill could.

While driving, a thought popped in my head: Could something else have caused this ear fluid? My emotions were all over the place. I hadn't been able to sleep at night, so I dragged myself from place to place during the day. The thought of food nauseated me.

I thought back to 2004 when my hearing fluctuated and I had lost more hearing. A key thing happened that year: I became a mom for the second time.

Less than two miles from the doctor's office, I made a bee-line for the pharmacy. I paid for a test, slid it in my purse, and got back behind the wheel.

After checking in at the doctor's, I dashed to the restroom. I unwrapped the white stick and did my urinary business.

"Mrs. Groves?" A lady in puke green scrubs held my medical chart. She called for me as I stepped out of the restroom.

Green Scrubs led us to a patient room.

"How are your ears?" She glanced at my chart.

"The same," I said.

Green Scrubs jotted a note on my chart.

"Okay, then," she said. "Let me take your vitals, and the doctor will be with you."

While waiting, the insides of my stomach felt like an imaginary roller coaster. With each breath I took, the roller coaster sped down its hill. My whole body flushed. The pits of my arms sweat. My temples pulsed and ached. The palms of my hands felt damp and cold.

"Hello, Mrs. Groves." A woman doctor I'd never met before walked into the room. "I'm filling in for your doctor today."

She stared at my chart and smiled. "Looks like we have something in common. I'm Dr. Groves."

I struggled to catch my breath. "I'm Shanna."

My hands were so clammy, I sat on them to keep them warm. In the mirror, I noticed my cheeks were flushed crimson red. Every time I swallowed, my tongue gagged, threatening to dry heave.

Dr. Groves looked up from my chart. "Okay, Shanna. What's going on with your ears?"

Before I could swallow, the words that kept racing through my brain like an invisible wrecking crew blurted out. "I'm pregnant."

Dr. Groves' head shot up. "You're..."

"I took a test." The words rolled out. "In the waiting room, I went to the restroom and took it. I wasn't planning this. I'm nervous and shocked and kind of relieved."

"Relieved?" she said.

My whole body shook as sentences flew out of my mouth. "That's why my ear clogged. That's what causes my hearing problems. That's why I am hard of hearing. Having babies. That's why I can't hear. Something happens to my hearing when I have babies."

"You're telling me you're pregnant?"

"Yes!"

"Well...congratulations."

∼

Two days later, I stood on a stage holding a microphone. I barely made it up the steps in my two-inch heels and constant state of vertigo. Although it was a relief to know why I couldn't hear, I was terrified about what I was going to say on that stage.

The week before my latest round of hearing problems, I fired off an e-mail to the pastor of my church. In it, I detailed the miraculous way in which God had restored my hearing in

New Jersey. It included the verses from the book of James that Pastor Rambo quoted during the healing prayer. My pastor urged me to share my story with the entire church during a Sunday testimony time.

No one knew I was pregnant, except Ron and Hannah, whom I called after leaving Dr. Groves' office. As my hearing problems persisted, Hannah insisted I still had to step foot on the stage and tell the story. A healing had happened in New Jersey. Even though the healing lasted a month — enough time for me to get pregnant — it still happened. The results from my latest hearing test proved it.

I stood behind the pulpit and gripped the microphone stand.

"I'm Shanna, and I want to tell you about the power of prayer in my life."

Waves of nausea flowed through me as the stage lights shone bright in my face.

"I have progressive hearing loss. It was diagnosed after the birth of my first child. Each year, I'd head to the audiologist to have my hearing tested. Each year, I'd have more loss."

Standing there in heels, the balls of my feet ached.

"A few weeks ago, I lost my little sister. Janie died on February 9 of this year. She was twenty-nine years old."

The auditorium lights dimmed with the only spotlight in that enormous room beaming on me.

"In a way, I had been grieving even before Janie died. Each year that I lost more hearing, I grieved the loss of my former life. My life with normal hearing. The life I wished I had. I desperately wanted to hear my kids' voices clearly.

"So when I got a chance to have someone pray with me, pray that my hearing would be restored, I was doubtful at first. Doctors heal people, not prayers. I was skeptical up until the pastor at my friend's church prayed for me and read James 5:13-15."

My Bible lay open in front of me on the pulpit. I pointed to the three verses in James underlined in pen.

"Is any one of you in trouble?" I read. "He should pray. Is anyone happy? Let him sing songs of praise. Is any one of you sick? He should call the elders of the church to pray over him and anoint him with oil in the name of the Lord. And the prayer offered in faith will make the sick person well; the Lord will raise him up."

I gazed at the dimly-lit audience.

"My ears had been sick for years, and I was sick with worry. How could I be a good mom without the ability to hear my kids? The pastor's prayer became my prayer. I didn't want to struggle to hear my kids anymore. I didn't want to live with the fear that one day I could wake up deaf. I wanted God's peace."

I took a deep breath.

"God healed me that day."

As my wobbly feet exited the stage, the crowd applauded. As I sat down next to Ron and Nicklaus in the front row, thoughts rolled through my mind. God had healed me, but not in the way I wanted. He lifted my hearing loss for a short time, only to allow it again. I knew why.

A baby grew inside me. I knew nothing about this child except for the day in which he or she was due to be born. Dr. Groves had calculated the week I had missed my period and added up the months of a full-term pregnancy. The due date was Christmas day.

Hearing loss or not, I was this child's mom.

A lip-reading mom.

Epilogue - A Letter to my Children

I t's time to 'fess up, kids. My ears aren't as sensitive as they used to be.

I confess I pretend to hear everything you say even when you're calling each other stupid, and I'm not sure that's what you said.

I confess I laugh before a joke's punch line, not because of a warped sense of humor, but because I didn't catch the joke's first sentence.

I confess I am unable to hear the telephone ring without my hearing aids.

I confess I don't understand most dialogue on TV without the closed-captioned turned on. I confess I get irked when the closed-captioning isn't working or is turned off.

I confess most people I haven't seen in years are shocked when I tell them I have to read lips to "hear" them.

I confess I rely on you to be my ears in the following situations: when a person asks me a question and I don't respond; when someone knocks softly at my door and I don't answer it; when the phone rings and I'm not wearing my hearing aids; when your baby brother wakes from his nap upstairs and is crying at the top of his lungs; when anything in the house beeps.

I confess I have learned to accept my limitations. I will never be successful in making a phone call to your dad or grandparents or anyone without some sort of special accommodations. Texting, amplified phones, and phone captioning are my new best friends.

I confess being a mom with hearing loss can be scary. When I attempt to lip-read your tiny mouths in the rearview mirror as I'm cruising seventy miles an hour down the highway, I dread fender benders or worse.

I confess being your mom makes me smile sometimes, especially when you throw temper tantrums in the store, whine for a new toy, or call me names I can't hear. My hearing aids have an on/off switch, and I utilize it frequently.

I confess having hearing loss is not normal to me. From the time you were born and I held you in my arms, my ears rang like sirens. All you have ever known, is a mom you must repeat things to three or four times. This is normal to you. But for the twenty-seven years preceding your birth and my hearing-loss diagnosis, I experienced something different: Ears that could hear.

I confess I rely much more on my eyes. When I open them wide, I see things clearly and can focus on reading your lips. When my eyes are shut, I feel lost.

I confess being a lip-reading mom has changed me. I'm not as quick to judge others who are different than me. I'm not as impatient. I don't get as frustrated with having to repeat things to a store cashier, wait in a long grocery line with a screaming child, or navigate the rearview mirror while reading your lips in rush-hour traffic.

I hope you understand.

MORE GREAT BOOKS FROM CROSSRIVERMEDIA.COM

THE UNRAVELING OF REVEREND G
RJ Thesman

When Reverend G hears the devastating diagnosis — dementia with the possibility of early-onset Alzheimer's — she struggles with the pain of forgetting those she loves and the fear of losing her connection with God. But she soon discovers there's humor to be found in forgetting part of the Lord's Prayer and losing a half-gallon of ice cream. And she discovers that while the question she wants to ask is, 'Why,' the answer really is, 'Who.'

WHILE THE GIANT IS SLEEPING

Alycia Holston, author / Suzi Stranahan, illustrator

An eagle builds her nest nearby, cars whiz past on the way to visit friends, and the Missouri River cuts through the landscape...all while the giant sleeps. In this delightful tale, author Alycia Holston and illustrator Suzi Stranahan introduce you to the Sleeping Giant of Helena, Montana, who slumbers while the world continues to grow and change around him.

THE BENEFIT PACKAGE
Thirty days of God's goodness from Psalm 103
Tamara Clymer, editor

Love, redemption, mercy, provision, revelation and healing... In Psalm 103, David listed just a few of the good things God did for him. These thirty devotionals, based on his list, will remind you that when circumstances overwhelm you - just unwrap His Benefit Package and rediscover God's goodness.

CPSIA information can be obtained at www.ICGtesting.com
Printed in the USA
LVOW05s1502230314

378574LV00023B/767/P